Praise for Higher Purpose

"Keith Hanna brilliantly articulates the connection between values driven business strategy and successful enterprises. Keith's refreshing insight and stories will inspire you to shape and understand your company's higher purpose and personality. Although creating meaningful work and customer experiences are not easy to quantify in a financial statement it will surely be businesses that ignore their values that will quickly become ignored by their customers and staff. The implications are astounding and profound."

Doug McNabb
President, Fabutan
www.fabutan.com

"Keith Hanna is provocative, challenging, and provides a fresh, enlightening, and holistic perspective for entrepreneurs in today's changing world. If you are committed to finding fulfillment that goes beyond making money, to looking at success in new ways, and to reaching for deeper meaning and lasting satisfaction in your work, then you will find value in what Keith has to say."

David Irvine,
Best selling author, *Simple Living In A Complex World*
www.davidirvine.com

"Keith Hanna will be the catalyst for shifting your business focus from being stressed and reactive to being more satisfied and proactive. His ability to activate your business success is a return on your time, energy and money investment that you cannot afford to miss. He has helped us focus on our higher purpose of assisting sales entrepreneurs in building confidence and building sales."

Tim Breithupt
Best Selling Author, *Take this Job and Love it!*
www.spectrain.com

"Companies die and wonder why. They had great business models, financial backing, a market wanting their product. What could possibly be missing? They didn't have heart. If there is not a match between the purpose of the leader and their business it's destined to be average at best! Matching head and heart is the gift that 'Higher Purpose, Higher Profit' brings to the table. Read the book cover to cover. Then go back and read it one section at a time and put thought to action. Watch your personal and professional purpose reap the rewards!"

R.W. (Bob) Johnson
President and Coach, Leader Search Inc.
www.leadersearch.com

"Over the past fifteen years I've watched Keith progress from keen student to thoughtful teacher. He has wrestled with success and emerged victorious, his journey made simpler along the way by an interesting discovery: success is dependent on recognizing who you are. 'Higher Purpose, Higher Profit' is a treat to read. Like having a good compass, it's easy to take a moment, check your course and correct if necessary."

Craig Riley
Venture Capitalist

"Fine business and personal coaching is a combination of technical and artistic skill - not unlike being a gifted musical conductor. Both professions take an excellent ear, a creative soul and a disciplined mind. This is the way Keith Hanna leads his clients far beyond the broader understanding and clearer direction of their lives and careers to the actual manifestation of their very purpose for being in business. By assisting us to align the components of our mission, values, needs, strengths and skills he thus assures the creation of business virtuosos. Bravo!"

Brian Copping
Personal Development Trainer

"Working with Keith Hanna and his insightful, provoking program enabled my company to grow in a positive, prosperous direction. It allowed me the clarity to know who I am as a business person, the insight to attract to my business the ideal clients and the motivation to create a joyful and productive workplace."

Harry Taylor
Chartered Accountant
www.HarryTaylor.com

"You will find Keith Hanna's writings and work to be sophisticated yet thoughtful. He will help you to dig deep, think, and figure out your own core values and how that affects every part of your life, especially your business. Keith has helped me to find the gaps I once had in my company, fill them with insightful knowledge, and let me build upon it through values, spirit, and intellect."

Sharlene Massie
Founder and CEO, About Staffing Ltd. Personnel Services
www.aboutstaffing.com

"'Higher Purpose, Higher Profit' is not a contradiction in terms. Each chapter of this little book sends out a big message. Refreshing and perceptive, Keith Hanna has drawn from his own loves, life and adventures to craft these engaging observations. Provocative, but not preachy, Keith helps the reader to reach their own conclusions and discover their own purpose. Keith shows us that there is a lot more to profit than money."

Tim Phillips
President, The Fore Front Group
Web-enabled Construction Services
www.forefrontgroup.com

"Words are strong tools. The combination of words in ways that communicate your true intentions is a wonderful skill and attribute. Keith Hanna possesses both. As my coach, Keith has helped me to identify my core values and beliefs and incorporate them into my business model. With a common purpose identified and shared with my team, my work with Keith helps keep me focused on both my personal and business visions, which can only make me more efficient."

Sharon Kaczkowski
President, Kaczkowski Occupational Therapy Consulting

"Keith Hanna has had a profound impact on my life. I can directly attribute a substantial increase in my revenues to our coaching work. More importantly however is the profound impact that our work together has had in my personal life. Never before have I had such a clear understanding of what drives me: the key to the puzzle if you will. The potential of this knowledge and how it will benefit me in the future is unimaginable. 'Higher Purpose, Higher Profit' suggests higher incomes, but effectively helps us to become better people who just happen to make more money as a result. "

Chad Sartison
Financial Planner

"Keith was the first to teach me the importance of analyzing user needs. Then when I thought I knew them, he stood his ground and insisted I study them even more. His methodical yet passionate approach to design always results in something better than what you started with. The information in this book is essential to any entrepreneur in search of their core values, a higher understanding of enterprise design, and the high road to success."

Randy Marsden
President, Madentec Assistive Technologies
www.madentec.com

"Keith has helped me get clear about who I am, and the value I bring to people. From this clarity comes an energy and that energy translates into positive action in the world. Entrepreneurism is all about discovering your gifts and bringing them out into the world so others can benefit and Keith provides the tools to go digging for those gifts."

Grant R. Molyneux
Professional Fitness & Lifestyle Coach
www.vitalize.ca

"In 'Higher Purpose, Higher Profit', Keith Hanna adeptly identifies and articulates, in his highly readable and entertaining style, how and why the most successful entrepreneurs succeed and profit in their business ventures. Through the vehicle of their commercial offering, each of these individuals passionately pursues his or her unique purpose and vision and thereby contribute greatly to their chosen market; and their customers recognize and appreciate their gift. Any entrepreneur who wishes to optimize the success of his or her business will benefit from the wisdom and know-how presented throughout this breakthrough book."

Peter Stewart
Partner, Stewart and Stewart Personal Law Services

"In this book, Keith explores the psyche of the entrepreneur. We are not just driven by a desire for profit. True happiness is derived from the creative and challenging process of building something meaningful. Keith's bite size stories and anecdotes focus on the human side of everyday business and personal life. He analyses the experiences that entrepreneurs routinely enjoy and endure with a mixture of technology, psychology, and humor. His unique perspective helps in achieving a more rewarding balance in life."

Steve Remmington
President, Entero Corporation
www.entero.com

"My work with Keith has helped me to reduce costs with efficient marketing and client contact systems and improve the quality of the facilitation and training that I deliver to clients. By obtaining clarity on my natural gifts and talents and what is holding me back, I have discovered how I can better serve my clients, improve a small piece of the world and live a balanced life while still honoring my values. I have made courageous steps forward in my business and life that I would never had made without the coaching and support. Because I am clear about who I am and who my core clients are, I am comfortable turning down work if it isn't aligned with my strengths and expertise."

Valerie MacLeod
Business Consultant and Facilitator
www.csmintl.com

"Having just started reading Keith's work only six months ago, I have quickly gained a wonderful clarity about how to better care for the needs of my own family and clients. Learning to live my values and create my ideal life has been a guiding principle in my own work and Keith's insights can provide you with a simple framework to properly focuses on your goals and accelerate your achievements. I have tremendous respect for Keith's written work and designs. His gift is the grounding he provides when you act on his inspired, common sense approach to life. You are going to love this book."

Richard W. Burley
President and Coach, iNTELECHi Inc.

"Keith Hanna's intuitive communication skills, bridging left and right brain activity, allow him to reduce entire complex thoughts and concepts to single words and simple statements. In assisting me to focus on Higher Purpose, Keith has coached me to Higher Profit and greater freedom."

Vincent T. Robichaud
CLU, CFP

"When we come to the forks on our Path of Life, we think deeply, consult with others or go with the flow, jumping in with both feet, head first or just dipping our toe – all for the sake of discovering which path to take. What's the big deal? It's big because we all know at a gut level that we are supposed to be doing something more meaningful, with more purpose. My greatest fear is realizing at age 70 what I should have been doing the previous 40 years. Having spent time with Keith, I now know, in all simplicity and with true clarity, the values I must honor to live my life so when I do reach 70, I will smile as I enjoy the feeling of fulfillment and having no regrets."

Gord Elser
Marketing and Promotions Strategist

"God has placed eternity in the hearts of mankind. Because of this, people desire the meaning of their gifts expressing in their lives and work. Keith has an incredible ability to help identify and draw out this significance, the traits in an individual that contribute so greatly to the feeling that "what my business does matters." He has helped me see new ways my enterprise can be an incredible vehicle to express the talents God has given me for the benefit of many – while making a return on my capital and the efforts of my staff."

Kent Davidson
President, Advanta Design Group
www.advantadesign.com

"Keith has been working with me and my team for the past two years, helping me escape the traditional role of 'Mr. Accountant.' We identified an important set of values and results and are moving forward as a team of agricultural support specialists assisting our noble farmers in fulfilling their life journeys and business goals. Keith has made an impact on my personal life as well, in my striving to improve balance."

Fred Mertz
Certified General Accountant, The Freedom Group

I have come to admire and appreciate Keith's intriguing and provocative powers of observation, insight and creativity. He ingeniously draws out the natural, but often ignored, dependence of profitability on personal and organizational values and purpose. Using carefully selected anecdotes Keith masterfully identifies, analyses and distills the key learnings which are a guide to integrity: the conscious alignment of shared principles and practices, beliefs and behaviours.

Glen Hay
Registered Architect

This book exemplifies the many ways in which Keith has positively impacted the lives of a great number of entrepreneurs. In the many years that I have known him, from struggling industrial designer and entrepreneur to today's wordsmith, his unabashed pursuit of elegance has been a cornerstone of his approach to life. He reminds us that thorough knowledge of self and the world, salted with a liberal dose of common sense, is a sure fire recipe for success. He is always thrilled at the success of his clients and colleagues.

Rod Burns
Professional Engineer and Venture Capitalist

After 21 years in dental practice, I finally found my self and my place in dentistry. I choose to serve my clients, team, family and myself with all the joy, connection, mutual trust and respect that is possible. Profoundly personal service is a richly-rewarding endeavour for the giver and the receiver. In order to get my life and business working so well in harmony, I have had to look inside and reach out for the support of others. Keith Hanna has been pivotal in helping me come out on my own and has a remarkable ability to assist entrepreneurs in connecting with who they are and what they have to offer.

Bill Cryderman
Holistic Dentist
www.drcryderman.com

Keith Hanna

Higher Purpose, Higher Profit tm

Putting Core Values Into Service

Venture Guiding Inc.

www.higherpurposehigherprofit.com

National Library of Canada Cataloguing in Publication Data:
A catalogue record for this publication is available from the
National Library of Canada.

Hanna, Keith Laird
    Higher Purpose, Higher Profit:
    Putting Core Values Into Service

ISBN 0-9730282-0-3

© 2002 Keith Laird Hanna

Published by Venture Guiding Inc.
Box 23165 Connaught
Calgary, Alberta, Canada
T2S 3B1
(403) 630 9413

keith@ventureguiding.com

Cover Design by Janine Mackinnon
janine@mackinnondesign.com

Edited by Wendy Ross

Printed in Canada by Blitzprint
www.blitzprint.com

"Higher Purpose, Higher Profit" is a trademark of Keith Laird
Hanna.

For my children, Kyle and Maren, the community of entrepreneurial activists and the future of this world.

General Contents

Detailed Contents

Foreword

There is a whole lot more to life than business, a whole lot more to business than profit and whole lot more to profit than money. The world of business is changing and one of the biggest and most profound changes is in human consciousness. Keith Hanna is at the leading edge of this change. The book that you now hold in your hands will take you to that edge and give you new perspectives that will change your business and your life.

As I have said and continue to say, Keith Hanna is a true blue guerrilla in every sense. He blends talent and energy with warmth and astonishing creativity. His knowledge of marketing and of business is extraordinary, yet he is able to combine that knowledge with genuine caring and humanity. His concept of "Higher Purpose, Higher Profit" is right on the money for entrepreneurs in our new millennium. It's not only right on the money, but right on the spirit and soul of a new way of doing business and life. I've always considered it a privilege to be connected with him in any way. And I consider it an equal privilege to be invited to write the foreword to his mind-boggling book.

The title of this book may cause you to believe that it is a new age book with new age ideas. Not true. It is an ageless book with timeless ideas...ideas that have been discarded and disregarded on our climb up the evolutionary ladder. The wisdom imparted in this book will take you to the frontier of a new way to live life and run your business. It will give new meaning, not only to your business mission, but also to the way you live your life. Ironically, while Keith's ideas might seem new, in truth, they reflect a wisdom as old as humankind itself. They are the things we all know deep down but often do not bring out. The realities of evolution and survival in the information age may have sidetracked us, but the home truths of living, working and building a business for a purpose higher than profit – while elevating those profits – are timeless.

This book strikes a delicate balance – balance between profits and human warmth, balance between technology and human caring, balance between company growth and human growth and balance between the practical and philosophical. It is written with vulnerability, warmth and compassion, the very qualities that lead in time to a more beautiful bottom line as well as a more beautiful life. Alive with anecdotes and stories about the people in Keith's world, "Higher Profit, Higher Purpose" is as fascinating and fun as it is enlightening and empowering. Keith reaches way down into his own soul to communicate with and uplift your soul.

In this book, you'll gain a whole new perspective on the role of humanity and spirituality in marketing and running a business. Your new enlightenment will contribute in a meaningful way to your bottom line as well as your inner self. It will be apparent both to your accountant and to your customers and employees. As obvious as it might be, the deeper meaning of life and business is all too often overlooked in the day-to-day existence of business. As you embrace a higher purpose to blend with your desire to profit, and use your resources to fulfill the greater possibilities open to you, the entire world around you will be enriched as a result of your unique gifts. Higher profits seem to be a natural outgrowth of being sensitive to customer expectations, then meeting and exceeding them. The bottom line is easy to measure. Higher profits and true wealth occur inside of you, and in the experiences and results you create for your family, your employees and the people with whom you do business.

Is higher purpose compatible with higher profits? You won't even have to ask that question after you've completed this book.

Jay Conrad Levinson
Author, "Guerrilla Marketing" series of books
Marin County, California, December 3rd, 2001
www.jayconradlevinson.com

Introduction

This book is about innovation, what I call "higher purpose, higher profit", and more specifically about the meaningful design of your business and the rest of your life. I have written this book for people who practice in the professional services or in any high-service-content business: sole practitioners, small partnerships, management teams and enterprising leaders working to change and improve the way their businesses and lives work. I am typically most attracted to and thus I have chosen my topics and language for people who are sophisticated, bold, accountable and collaborative. I love the English language, irony and ideas of great worth and merit and I hope this shines through the text.

The central theme of this book, while clearly stated in the idea that "personal values result in economic value" nevertheless has a rich, emotional foundation. I decided early on that the best way to develop the theme was to unfold it through a series of perspectives. There is already too much hype parading around as facts so I have drawn heavily from my own experiences and the people I have worked with. I like to think of the subject of this book as if it were a rare jewel, held in a multifaceted room with one hundred windows. The view through each is unique and a complete understanding comes only from a complete set of views. Inside is a mysterious widom that I think we all share, that we all pursue and that many of us hope to fulfill before we die. I am among many people who have written about these very same ideas through the ages and my humble aim is to put my own spin on them and package them for use in the development of the professional service business, the domain in which I have chosen to play. In that approach, I believe I am working in a frontier.

As a designer at heart, I have taken a designer's approach to both the content and layout of the book. This work is a synthesis from a great many sources and I have referenced them directly in the text where they are signficant. I respect that the audience for my coaching services and for this book are busy people, so I have designed the booked to fit in to a hectic life. This means that I have paid attention to the user interface, the design and flow of the information and the quality of the user experience. I hope the final product is both easy to access and generates a great experience. I have made it possible for you to read it in a number of different ways, depending on your purpose and reading style. The book features one hundred chapters, split into four equal sections based on my four core values. I have dedicated each chapter to an idea linked, in some interesting fashion, back to the main theme. The layout is random-access and you can read the essays in any sequence and over any duration and get value from them. You can read one chapter or all one hundred or any in between. You can read all four sections or just the ones that interest you. You can start at the beginning, in the middle or read them back to front. You can read one every morning or evening to support one hundred days of change. You can read one every week to help ground your weeks for two years. The book fits on the back of most toilets in any orientation because that is where many entrepreneurs do their reading. I have started with a manifesto that neatly summarizes the one hundred points I make in the body of material that follows. You can read that first or only. Anyway that works for you works for me.

This is not a how-to book in the traditional sense, although I do present some means to achieving higher personal and economic value. It is also a why-to. I am interested in the context for this work and the meaning of the good deeds we perform in business and life. Ultimately, my calling is to lend whatever support I can to the enterprise of making ventures work better for entrepreneurs and the world around them. I hope that I might make even a hint of that contribution to you.

Keith Hanna
Bragg Creek, Alberta, January 31st, 2002
www.ventureguiding.com

Higher Purpose, Higher Profit

Manifesto
Personal Values Result in Economic Value

1   Personal values result in economic value.

2   Authentic products and services create a meaningful experience that nourishes the souls of a new kind of customer seeking a deeper relationship with the companies that serve them.

3   As we look inside to find the deeper meaning of our lives, we can find the inspiration to transform our ventures from mere profit-seeking vehicles to grander instruments of social and environmental change.

4   A transparent brand is an authentic statement of core values that drives the creation of everything that a company is and stands for; it is not just about marketing but how a company fulfills the values implied by the marketing.

5   A focused definition of the ideal client is neither too narrow nor too broad and provides a lifetime of opportunities to create high value services.

6   As we rise above the facade of rhetoric, the opacity of jargon and the inhumanity of hubris, we say something interesting and personal about why we are really in business.

7   Great service builds a platform for long-term trust, permanent high-margin purchasing and frequent good referrals; great service providers suspend their self-interest to do the things that really touch their clients and their clients respond with their loyalty and evangelism.

8   The best questions inspire a deep personal introspection about what matters most in life and invoke powerful insights buried under the surface of the urgent daily grind.

9   A person who has found home on the stage of their life is a bright light for others to see their own.

10   Each of us needs some combination of teamwork, partnership or exquisite self-care and mastery to balance the different energies that must flow into the productive building and operation of our ventures.

11   Authenticity reflects the meaningful connection customers have with a company that is more important than the basic technical quality of its products.

12   The best marketing is not a description of product features and technology that no one will care about in four business quarters; the best marketing engages customers in a meaningful conversation about what everyone cares most about, has cared most about and will care most about.

13   The source of all joy and stress lies in the creation or destruction of core values, what is most important to us, what we stand for and what drives us forward in our entrepreneurial pursuits.

14   Authentic self-expression is a lifelong journey, made humble by the awesome power of the creative source and joyful by the simple grace of well-chosen words.

15   Doing business in ways that reflect the life purpose and core values of people that work in and on an enterprise is more attractive and more deeply satisfying to its customers than the commodities it makes and sells.

16   As we come to accept our own faults and flaws, and those of the people around us, we release more of our value into the world.

17   We are accountable for all errors for which we personally pay a price, not because we or someone else is to blame but simply because our clients expected more from us.

18   Solid ground is a strong set of affirmative beliefs that supports everyone on the team to find productive outlets for the fulfillment of their driving needs.

19 Myths and stories can be more effective than procedure manuals in teaching new staff about the rich patina and deep heritage of valuable learning residing in the culture of the enterprise.

20 When we reframe threatening situations, we overcome the fear that prevents us from exploiting important opportunities to get our needs met constructively, in the service of others.

21 Systems of single-source accountability make it very clear to everyone on a team who owns a result and therefore who has the ultimate authority to decide how that result will come to be.

22 Affirmative beliefs play out as constructive results and experiences and eventually reverse the pattern of the self-limiting thoughts and miserable outcomes they imply.

23 A venture type that honours an entrepreneur's creative and growth orientation is easier, more fun and less stressful to create and manage successfully.

24 When we use first-person, affirmative, grounded, present-tense and active voice, we feel powerful, establish powerful intentions and create powerful results.

25 When we find the courage to engage the possibilities life has for us, we move past our fears and create lives rich with meaning and fulfillment that inspire other people to do the same.

26 Each company endures the disintegrating forces of changing technology, intensifying competition and whimsical customers by building an attractive brand, agreeable culture, deliverable system, satisfying product and profitable capital structure.

27 Ultimately we cannot fake or manufacture the meshing of values between company and client; we can only sort the clients who are naturally motivated by our value set from the clients who are not.

28 Our best prospective clients, just like our best prospective romantic mates, are those candidates with whom we have the most intimate meshing of core values and the best DNA connection.

29 A modular approach allows a service provider to make some reasonable assumptions about what most people need, build some standard discrete modules and then assemble them in unique ways to meet the differing needs of each customer.

30 Stakeholder feedback and input during the design process move us out of fantasy and arrogance and into making our ventures work better for buyers, sellers, servers, users and funders.

31 True power comes not from lone entrepreneurs wielding their creative authority on the naked world but from the grace and courage of a large group of supporters making a safe and stable platform on which to launch their dreams.

32 We close more sales from a place of faith than from a place of doubt and fear.

33 When our ground is strong, we have taken a predominance of workable positions that support us to create the positive results we intend, with the support of the people in our presence.

34 The form of well-designed service reflects its function to deliver on its underlying value proposition.

35 A product that is at once a useful tool offering great utility, an evocative work of art offering great beauty, an informative symbol offering great self-expression and an inviting portal offering great access is more valuable than a basic technical commodity.

36 Good corporations treat each job like a product designed to meet the special needs of its consumer – a powerful employee who has the ultimate power to change vendors if the quality, service and price do not fit his or her needs.

37 When people buy into the larger world view and deeper spirit of the enterprise, they form an interconnected community of loyal supporters actively working to expand the community by enrolling more people.

38 Samples of high-price, high-passion services lower the perceived risk of purchase by creating strong emotional connections between the buyer and service provider.

39 When we speak from the heart, about what is most important to us, the right people listen, the right people show up and the right people buy.

40 Good sales people empower their prospects to make choices that work for them by being both respectful and enthusiastic.

41 Ironically, businesses work better when the founders make themselves redundant and install all of the good will, key business relationships and intellectual property into the business structure.

42 If we ask the "why" and "how" questions of function before the "what" and "which" questions of form, we have the best chance of reconciling our values and creating a shared vision that honors everyone without compromise.

43 The next wave in the economy is the reconciliation of modern and post-modern ways – a hybrid approach that balances the best of the old and new.

44 By defining our ventures according to our unique contributions and core clients we are free to design an endless series products that extend the lifetime value of our client base.

45 Entrepreneurs who overcome the trust and communication barriers to distributive collaboration access the wealth of intellectual and human capital held in the network of their people.

46 A good tagline reflects who we are, attracts the best clients and spreads like a virus.

47 In the end, we matter, not because we can prove that we do, but because we are members of a powerful collective consciousness that continues to shape the experiences of all of us, largely for the better.

48 When a company consistently lives up to the promise of the values implied by its world view, the company earns the loyalty of its high value customers, repeat business, forgiveness for its errors and protection from the lure of competitors.

49 We can solve sometimes serious business problems by learning to listen to and interpret the personal feedback our physical bodies are giving us.

50 Our real legacy is the love we leave behind when we are gone: a world that works better not just for our friends and family, but for everyone who has yet to be born.

51 It is often more enjoyable, faster and more efficient to build a business with many smaller steps than to bolt forward and burnout with fewer larger and more strenuous steps.

52 Real leadership comes from people who are clear about what they want and find the courage inside to stand up and ask for it.

53 Faced with their own demise, people show amazing abilities to find solutions. Breaching an impasse, whether in the wilds of nature or in business, is sometimes just a matter of moving tiny steps forward, steps that can radically alter the landscape of possibilities.

54 An organic planning process unfolds with a fluid and conscious enterprise, balancing the enduring character of its purpose and values with the continuously evolving environment of its technologies, customers and competitors.

55 No matter how successful we get, the conditions upon which we base our success are sure to change: there is always somewhere to go, something to learn and some improvement to make in the continual process of personal and business evolution.

56 The strength of our convictions and the power of our forward progress reveal the secrets to our future success, many of which are unknowable at the time of commitment.

57 Service providers can leverage their time by methodically building a foundation for increasingly valuable phases of growth.

58 A sustainable growth company maintains a strong brand, a sweeping long-term vision, high margins and a loyal customer base assuring that the business will endure well past the death of its founder.

59 We sometimes fail to see opportunity because it comes disguised as something uncomfortable or terrifying or tragic, and not as something packaged with a warm invitation and an obvious welcome.

60 In any enterprise, we must rise out of blind faith through crises of faith, on our way to building a conscious faith and confidence in ourselves and others.

61 In the context of a quickly unfolding, ambiguous future, a good decision is one that gets made and one where the results of error are recoverable.

62 While it seldom works to be last-to-market, it is more lucrative to be the best-to-market than to be the first-to-market and the first-to-fail.

63 When we create a vision in alignment with our true personal values and not with social defaults, we find that we have ample motivation to navigate any problems on our path to fulfillment.

64 What we learn from rapidly building and testing new service prototypes in real time are the secrets to making the proposed venture more attractive, agreeable, deliverable, satisfying and profitable.

65 Breaking new ground with highly personal and intangible services in a frontier market is probably the most challenging and thus least crowded opportunity to create new business and ease reliance on referrals.

66 An innovation is often the result of many iterations of dedicated art and science getting closer and closer to some new working idea and important breakthrough.

67 Forward progress through a seemingly impossible crisis does not result from the distraction of obsessing on failure but from a focus on and faith in some unforeseen path to safety and success.

68 It is only through conscious living that we come to appreciate the value of life, its passing and our continuity in some eternal flow – the feeling of timeless, spaceless bliss.

69 Great guides, whether in the ventures of nature or business, remember where their people want to go, possess a sophisticated set of tools to get there and bring a hard-won experience in route finding, hazard evaluation and risk management.

70 A smooth sales process is a graduating process of many small steps, each with the intention of increasing trust and commitment towards a mutually beneficial commercial relationship.

71 A business endures, past its startup and again through the transitions dictated by a rapidly changing business environment, by striking a balance between the chaos of good leadership and the order of good management.

72 Every result, whether positive or negative, is the net effect of all negative and positive intentions, beliefs and attitiudes that accumulate and build momentum through time.

Higher Purpose, Higher Profit

73 Prior to the onslaught of a prolonged creative draught and its resulting addictive behaviour, we all have the opportunity to reach out for the support we need to maintain and continually recommit to the full potential we have as creative beings.

74 When we overcome our limiting beliefs and connect to our more empowering beliefs, we behave in ways that add genuine value and make life and business easier, more fun and more lucrative.

75 As we make commitments and set action steps that stretch our zones of comfort we create the positive experience of moving forward and fulfilling the promise of our core values.

76 By focusing on clients with the most stressful problems and the most resources to solve them, we build strong, healthy businesses that can spread the wealth to others who are less fortunate.

77 We create a positive experience for our customers by using our talents to remove the stress caused by the absence of a core value we share.

78 If we choose clients that appreciate our core values and then design and operate our businesses based on these same values, we will naturally create more valuable results that warrant premium prices.

79 We do not know how much time we each have, but we can know that in every moment we are living good lives and making a difference.

80 We are motivated to serve others and create value simply because we have been hurt in the precise area in which we seek to make a difference.

81 As we grow as entrepreneurs and continue to support our people with valuable new innovations, they continue to support us with permanent streams of revenue.

82 If we were all paying more taxes, it would mean that we were creating more value and abundance for ourselves and the rest of the country.

83 Ironically, it is more fulfilling to give away what we ourselves need because it requires that we take action to constructively create the same experiences that we want from others.

84 Conversation is a great way to learn about people, to discuss different points of view and to ultimately reconcile them in the form of a high-end purchase.

85 Giving thanks is a way for us to honour the people who participate in our personal lives and business ventures and to strengthen the community of supporters who are vested in our best interests.

86 Spending and not hoarding whatever it is we want more of puts us back into the natural flow of what was, what is and what will be.

87 As we continue to expand the problem space, finding ever more complex and stressful situations to solve, we earn higher pay as our share of the greater results we generate by solving them.

88 A service that returns many times its price back in tangible, measurable results is an investment that justifies a higher price, not an expense that prompts price objections.

89 An integrated service program is a package of solutions that has greater value than time sold by the hour.

90 By refusing to do penance for sins against standards we do not choose as our own, we set forth a powerful mechanism of goodwill that invites all manner of prosperity and good times.

91 As consumers, we reward companies which reflect our values and offer meaningful products and services by paying premium prices and remaining loyal.

92 It is confidence – our spiritual connection to our creativity – that is the precondition of creating the successful track record that most clients need before buying in to something new.

93   Well-designed products and services balance the latest in technological advances with the very personal needs of the human beings using them.

94   The most vital businesses rise above the technicalities of their operations to engage people in a deeper conversation about what matters most in life and the enterprise of making their way in the world.

95   The more we reflect emotional content – the authentic aesthetic value – in every detail of our ventures, the more people are moved to buy, invest in, be a part of and use what we offer.

96   Greatness comes not from an absense of errors but from a magnificent response to them.

97   Fulfillment is not the result of distantly-spaced and short-lived achievements but the experience of ideal days borne of patient, conscious design.

98   Our best contributions to our best people are really profound acts of love which improve their worlds and make our ventures healthier, stronger and capable making an even bigger difference.

99   The greatest gift that we have to give is the contribution we are alive to make.

100   Ethical profit is both a company's reward for its ingenuity and a statement by its employees, investors and customers of their commitment to the more noble purpose and values at the heart of the enterprise.

Higher Purpose, Higher Profit

Part I: Authenticity
Learning What is Most Important

Creating Clarity and Higher Quality

Putting Core Values into Service

In the latter part of the 1980s, on a visit to a coffee shop near the Pike Street market in Seattle, I had the opportunity to try a new beverage: a cup of vanilla steamed milk. I had never heard of Starbucks before then, never had a cup of coffee and never had occasion to enter a coffee shop for that matter, but this beverage and this place was a genuinely novel experience for me.

Years ago, when I started my coaching business, I had a grungy, guerrilla-type office, carpeted with old green shag carpet. While it fit my budget well, I avoided meeting clients there, especially potential clients that I had never met or did not know well. I began inviting prospects to a coffee shop, where we could introduce ourselves, learn about each other and explore our possible business opportunities. I frequently chose Starbucks, the place most people seemed to prefer. It was always comfortable kicking back in a set of wing-back chairs, in a beautiful environment, next to a roaring fireplace, learning the details of someone's entrepreneurial passions and how I might assist them in creating more value for themselves and their customers.

Starbucks, for some reason, always felt like a good place to go to connect with people and to talk about what was most important to them and what they were trying to create in their ventures. I also liked Starbucks because it was the only high-end coffee shop that made a drink especially for me. I am allergic to milk and do not drink coffee and so the "soy chai latte" was an innovation that was respectful and inclusive and allowed me to participate in the new latte ritual.

What is always amazing to me is the phenomenon behind Starbucks. The drink I regularly buy is just under $5. This is just a beverage, but no one forces me go into a Starbucks and pay a premium for it. I do it willingly and with enthusiasm. And I am not alone.

People consume much more than a beverage when they buy from Starbucks. Howard Schultz acquired and grew the company to its present level of success and size based on a unique idea. As he told in his book *Pour Your Heart Into It*, as a young man, he always wanted to be a part of something great, to belong and to do something real. In the late 80s, people were tired of hanging out at the mall and were searching for a place other than the bar to connect with people. The notion of the "third place" arose to describe locations other than home and work that people would spend their social time. Starbucks naturally moved in to exploit this social change. As fine as their coffee might be, what Starbucks seems to be about and what people are really consuming is community. The difference between a $5 latte and a few cents of commodity materials is the unique contribution of community and the authentic experience that supports it: the true value of Starbucks.

Starbucks may be one of the first major public growth companies to become successful not on the strength of proprietary technology or strong national advertising, but on a platform of very personal core values. While Starbucks has been widely criticized for its ubiquity and sprawling growth – there are intersections in Vancouver where if the line is too long at one Starbucks, you can go across the street to a different one – no one is forcing people to go in and buy there. Whether you like the company or not, it is interesting to acknowledge their achievement. Starbucks means something to the people that work there and the millions of people who show up an average of eighteen times a month to buy there. By taking a stand for authenticity in its experience and respect for its people, Starbucks has parlayed a classic commodity into a high margin, high wealth and high value enterprise. *Personal values result in economic value.*

Embracing the Spirit of the New Customer

Abraham Maslow developed the now famous hierarchy of needs. The hierarchy places basic survival needs at the base of simple human existence and the pursuit of self-actualization at the pinnacle of human existence. The theory describes how people escalate the level of their existence by working through a process of scaled needs: when people have figured out how to dodge bullets, thatch a roof over their heads to keep out the rain and find a sustainable source of water and basic food, they can set about fulfilling more sophisticated need for social interaction and the pursuit of ever more meaningful experiences. According to Maslow, it is difficult for anyone to pursue the meaning of their life's calling if they are worried about being killed by thugs. Success at one level is the basis for learning to be successful at the next. Life is a process of climbing the stairs of the pyramid of need.

My own simplification of this concept is that people proceed from survival and security, through success, to meaning and purpose. I see society moving through the same three phases en masse. For at least the last decade, a new kind of customer has been emerging. The demographer Paul Ray labeled this new social group "cultural creatives." This group is roughly 20% of the population and is quite different from the "traditional" and "modern" groups that went before.

Traditionalists, who are about 30% of the population, are heartlanders who value family and simple living. They have their roots in the pre-industrial revolution time, up to about 1930, and, as a group, were invested in achieving survival and security for their families.

Modernists, at about 50% of the population, are primarily a post-war phenomenon, with roots dating back to the industrial revolution. For this group, the machine age and science brought incredible levels of prosperity and success, but also the eventual loss of human and environmental values. This movement started to wane in the ultra-materialistic '80s. During that decade, as more people achieved material success, millions of people became unfulfilled by their achievements and began searching for deeper meaning. Enter the cultural creatives.

The New Economy has been dubbed the information age, the creative age, the post-industrial age or the service age; it is really the age of experience. While the purchase and use of manufactured objects and "hardware" dominated the modern age, this age seems to be more about "software." Where acquisition and ownership and the satisfaction of more material needs was predominant, there is now an increasing emphasis on the quality of experience. We cannot take our money and things with us, but our prosperity has made a new life possible.

Meaningful experience is the pinnacle of human existence and what the new creative customers demand. We can all keep and enjoy our comfortable homes, nice cars, fancy clothes and all the other accoutrements of success, but a deeper satisfaction awaits from companies savvy to the need for deeper meaning.

We all supply a service or product that offers definite material satisfaction, but this technical level of practice is not the highest and best of what we are capable of creating. There is something spiritual as well. We can also deliver the experience of fun, drama, connection, challenge, intimacy, discovery, control, beauty, loyalty, integrity, trust, community, celebration, acknowledgment, recognition, excitement, humour or passion. *Authentic products and services create a meaningful experience that nourishes the souls of a new kind of customer seeking a deeper relationship with the companies that serve them.*

Entrepreneurial Activism 3
Making Personal Innovation the Precedent for Global Innovation

Two of the most significant social innovators of the twentieth century have strikingly similar thoughts regarding the path of widespread world change. Mahatma Gandhi's famous guide "be the change you wish to see in the world" defines the need to change one's self before being in a position to change the world. He is proof of the Ayn Rand notion that one person with a well-placed lever can change the world. Similarly, Nelson Mandela has made very clear connections between the years he spent imprisoned and the movement he eventually led. The value of his years locked away in an indifferent prison cell, was the time he had to change himself from an angry and hateful young man into a wise and reflective one. Although he has always been quick to humbly point out that he was only the most visible part of a very large collective working together to defeat Apartheid, his brilliant example has nonetheless inspired a generation of political activists who have seen very clearly that anyone can overcome oppression and make a difference. He did not change his country until he changed himself.

Political activism is an obvious mode of making change in the world but it is not the only way to develop, master and make a contribution to people and the greater planet. Everyday, millions of people volunteer their time and talents to a myriad of social causes that would be unviable and bankrupt if not for the contributions of armies of selfless people. Many others write checks towards these same causes using their wealth if not their time to shift problems to the affirmative. Indeed, with the twin forces of increasing misery in the world and increasing wealth amongst a new generation of technology entrepreneurs, philanthropy and volunteering are becoming more prominent engines of social innovation.

And a person does not have to forgo making a good living while making a difference. Beyond social activism, volunteerism and philanthropy is the idea of commercial enterprise. Businesses, both small and large are becoming significant drivers of the social and political landscape. What differentiates either entrepreneurs or intrapreneurs from these other change agents is a profit motive. Historically, this has been the primary purpose of business. But we appear to be in the process of some sort of economic enlightenment. Enterprising people, in search of greater meaning and fulfillment, and disillusioned by the cold processes of money making, are broadening their visions to reflect a more social and environmentally-centred world view. Just making money is ultimately a boring job. Making money and making a difference is interesting. People are pursuing a higher purpose and reaping the more fulfilling kind of profit that entails.

While there are problems in the world that would never get commercial attention because of prohibitive economics, there are a class of problems that get attention precisely because there is financial merit in doing so. Such opportunities are not morally inferior to the apparently more selfless social contributors. They are just on a different part of the continuum of contribution. Profits provide the resources to bring about change and to perpetuate innovation.

The path of entrepreneurship is itself the process of personal growth and mastery leading to global growth and mastery. Profit may be the measurement of business success but the pursuit of a grander purpose is the real point. There is a big need for enterprising people to join in the quest for better societies and a better world. *As we look inside to find the deeper meaning of our lives, we can find the inspiration to transform our ventures from mere profit-seeking vehicles to grander instruments of social and environmental change.*

Transparent Brands 4
Strengthening the Core Value Proposition

One of the first new products to come from Apple with the return of Steve Jobs was the iMac. In an interview with *Fast Company* magazine, Jonathan Ive, the industrial designer behind the iMac, articulated the design principles that drove its creation as "simplicity, accessibility, honesty and enjoyment." The striking features of the product and its successors are their transparent, multicoloured enclosures. This has become a house style at Apple with everything from workstations to laptops, and power adapters to cables coming in translucent packaging. But this physical transparency is not a vacuous fashion statement or a cute product design detailing. This approach is saying something very interesting about how people inside and outside of the company regard the company. Physical transparency is a metaphor for a transparent user experience; how the computer works is always obvious to the user. This is how people identify with Apple and what constitutes the open character of its brand. It is a good brand.

Social commentators have been increasingly vocal about the intrusion of global brands into the once quiet and pristine areas of our environment. Pejorative labels of people as "brand conscious" suggest a weakness in character: a breach of authentic life in favour of superficiality. It is true that our environment is smeared with logos. You cannot walk down any street, watch a movie or television or stroll through a park without seeing a Nike swoosh, a Tommy Hilfiger flag, the bright neon of Sony or the Marlborough Man on a horse during a cattle drive. Commercialism abounds. Brands rule, but there are ones that deliver on the values they imply and there are ones that do not.

Consider the branding of the Marlborough cigarette. The Marlborough Man is one of the strongest icons of American culture, evoking John Wayne and the steadfast, independent entrepreneur. I think that such brands reflect humanity's search for an expression of meaning. The symbols of the great companies become symbols of their values. At first glance, the Marlborough Man may seem to be an arbitrary semiotic expression of a dangerous and dirty personal habit, but it does mean steadfast independence and personal choice. This was what Phillip Morris, the man, was all about. And it is what the United States is about. That a large proportion of sales of Phillip Morris cigarettes come from the third world should be of no surprise. They have become an effective symbol of freedom and choice for nations emerging from poverty and oppression and seeking American-style democracy. These are values that many people identify with, but, unlike the iMac which actually delivers on its value proposition, a lifetime spent smoking Marlboroughs will ultimately destroy freedom and choice. Marlborough may mean something to its customers and reflects the values of its founders, but that reflection is artificial and superficial because the products ultimately fail to deliver on the values they seem to promise. Here, the brand and product are incongruent.

Apple has come to mean simplicity, accessibility, honesty and enjoyment. These are the values at their core. These values show up in the design of products and company culture. They allow staff, investors, customers and vendors to identify with the company and resonate with what is at the heart and soul of its creative process. Apple is a transparent brand because its values drive the creation of everything that Apple stands for. The Apple brand brands everything that is Apple. *A transparent brand is an authentic statement of core values that drives the creation of everything that a company is and stands for; it is not just about marketing but about how a company fulfills the values implied by the marketing.*

Sustainable Differentiation 5
Focusing on a Good Niche in the Market

As a part of our vision for an active lifestyle, my wife and I acquired two malamute puppies. Malamutes are an ancient northern dog breed with a long and decorated history and one of the first domesticated dog varieties in the canine genealogy. Their character evolved with the Mahlemut people of the North, and to this day they carry with them a special kinship with their human owners. Together man and dog braved harsh northern life, each relying on the other for survival.

Unlike most of their human counterparts, Malamutes have no doubt about their life purpose. They pull. Malamutes are sled dogs. Their proclivity to pull was evident from the moment we picked them up from the pet store, and they seem happiest when they are on a trail in front of our sled.

In the ecology of the natural world, species prevail by doing what they do best, varying their approaches and adapting by natural selection to niches created by changing geological or geographical conditions. Species flourish by striking a balance. Evolution seems to favour flexibility. There is a fine line between being too different and not different enough. According to fossil evidence presented by Steve Jones in *Darwin's Ghost*, the domestic dog split off from the wolf some ten thousand years ago and the coyote split off a million years ago. The wolf, chose a narrow strategy of living in packs and hunting big game, while the coyote developed a more flexible approach to the encroachment of humanity upon its habitat. Coyotes have thrived in the niches created by civilization, while the wolf has had a more difficult time and remains threatened to this day.

In the economic analog, an enterprise prevails by picking a flexible specialty in a business environment that is always changing with shifting competitors, drifting client requirements and emerging technologies. In my case, I am a coach, and I contribute innovation. This is how I "pull", but it is not a complete definition of my niche.

Purpose defines not just the special thing we do but the special people we do it for. If I say, "my market is everyone", which at first seems to make me open to opportunity, I will likely not be unique among my competitors. Such a broad intention would require that I find the lowest common denominator in a very large, undifferentiated market space – a compromise which would not lead to a highly satisfying and high-margin service. While it may be true that each of the six billion people walking the earth could benefit from the meaningful change brought on by an effective coaching relationship, it is doubtful that I would be able to craft a marketing message, sales pitch, product design, delivery method and pricing scheme that would satisfy everyone. People simply have different values, needs and preferences.

A sustainable market niche reflects a well-defined community of potential clients. I have always been attracted to entrepreneurs, and I have worked with all kinds in man-ufacturing, service and information businesses. I prefer working with high-service content businesses. Within that larger scope, I prefer working on restructuring successful established businesses rather than on emerging ones. Within that finer scope, I prefer working with professional services, with a high information content, requiring lots of training, an ethical framework and a serious approach to the business development problem. These criteria give me a basic ethnographic definition of my ideal client and my niche: "Established professional service entrepreneurs." While this definition limits the kind of clients I pursue, it helps me focus on the highest-value situations where my unique approach best fits. Ironically, there is an abundance of potential clients fitting my profile. *A focused definition of the ideal client is neither too narrow nor too broad and provides a lifetime of opportunities to create high value services.*

Marketing by Manifesto 6
Using Real Language for Real People

In *The Cluetrain Manifesto*, authors Levine, Locke, Searls and Weinberger argue for the existence of a new kind of market conversation. This conversation is no longer the one spoken in highly polished corporate prose through the metaphysical construct called a company. It is no longer about arcane technicalities and mundane product features. It is people speaking to people about what is most important to them. The conversation is not just human, it is valuable and purposeful.

Seth Godin, following on the work of Cluetrain, Richard Dawkins and others, introduced the notion of the "idea virus." An idea virus is an idea whose time has come and one which spreads geometrically through a population of subscribers. To Godin and his friend Jay Levinson, such an approach to marketing is far more powerful for the small business than an advertising-siege. In viral campaigns, customers enroll customers: an internet-enabled enhancement over word-of-mouth and network marketing. The idea virus is a manifesto or platform that attracts cool communities of dedicated customers actively engaged by the purpose and values of the company at its core.

Patagonia is an outdoor clothing company notable for its environmental design and the loyalty of its customers. For decades it has sat at the top of its industry with leading edge technology, advanced designs and high retail prices and margins. Its founder, Yvon Chouinard, has become an accidental prophet of the ideal of using business as a vehicle for social responsibility. His core purpose is to "use business to inspire and implement solutions to the environmental crisis." With this manifesto, he and his company have been changing the industrial paradigm of business having to choose between making money or making a difference. He has become wealthy, doing the social good.

One year, the company started offering organic cotton garments. To do this, years earlier, they had to seed a grassroots organic cotton farming movement. Such farmers were dedicated to growing cotton without pesticides, preventing a substantial amount of poison from leaching into the earth. The year that the products debuted – jeans, polo shirts and the like – the company introduced its spring catalogue with an essay about cotton dyeing. This is how the conversation went: OK Mr. Consumer, you are the one who determines whether environmental design is going to work by choosing to buy products like organic cotton garments. We have made the cotton friendly, but the dyes used to colour the products are harmful too. If we use vegetable dyes the colour fades quickly and the garments lose their aesthetic appeal and you will not buy them. If we use traditional dyes, we poison the earth. You are the consumer: which do you buy?

This situation was a very real design and marketing dilemma illustrating that it does not matter if a product does not harm the environment if no one buys it. Therein lies the compromise at the heart of the design and business problem.

The fascinating thing about this dialog is that it was not between a VP of product development and a VP of marketing. It was between a company that cared about something and its customers. It was not held in private strategy sessions but in public catalogues, stores displays and websites. It was not about the technology or product features it was about what a company stands for. It was about its core values, its higher purpose.

Most products come and go. Core values endure. *As we rise above the facade of rhetoric, the opacity of jargon and the inhumanity of hubris, we say something interesting and personal about why we are really in business.*

Overcoming Self-interest and Doing Right By People

As I began to gather momentum during the first few years of my coaching business, I found myself in front of many well-heeled clients. This obviously meant I would need to upgrade my wardrobe. On this point, I am in clear disagreement with Shakespeare's admonition to avoid any new ventures that require new clothes. As a designer, I look for any excuse to refurnish my closet. So, armed with a newly minted credit line, I embarked on the arduous task of renovating my attire.

I began my sartorial enterprise by exploring the various stores. In my city, there are a number of very good upscale men's retailers. At various stages in my professional life I had patronized all of them, but I had not yet dedicated myself to any particular one. I usually bought from a store that had the piece I liked and had very little connection to the store itself or the people that worked there.

As a designer, I had developed some very particular preferences and peculiar tastes, and so the process took a couple of seasons to complete. At the start of the process, I went into one of the stores, expecting the level of service boasted about by their ads and reputation for great service. I had a few genuinely good purchases there, but something had changed. I often shopped on Saturday and wore shorts and sandals. On at least three different occasions at this store, I watched in disbelief at sales person after sales person walking by me as if I were not there, as if I had no money. On each occasion I had to actually request help with getting my questions answered about certain garments I was interested in. Since I am in the coaching industry, I saw this as an opportunity to maybe make a contribution to this company. I made a call to their VP of operations who agreed to see me and hear my ideas for improving service. After confirming my appointment, I traveled for hours to meet the VP, only to find out, once I got there, that something more important had come up and he had not bothered to cancel or phone to reschedule. As I left their office, I saw a sign on the door that said something about building relationships. Whatever. Not in my experience. I fumed.

These days there is nothing more dangerous than poor service, especially consistently poor service. Customers who do not get treated well, get angry and tend to tell many other people. The Internet makes this ranting even easier with websites like planetfeedback.com and epinions.com. What is worse, for every complaint we hear about, there are many more lurking in the shadows.

The final time I strolled through this company's store I saw a beautiful overcoat. I saw the price tag and just did not have the confidence to buy it. One year later I began focusing my purchases at another store and got to know Derik Simpson pretty well. I told him of my saga with the other firm in town and the overcoat that I really liked, that I could not justify and which was now gone. One day, I came in to pick up an item that had been hemmed, and he called me over to a table. He laid out a beautiful overcoat that was very similar to the one I had let go. This one belonged to another customer, but Derik said that if I liked the style, he had found one in my size on the discount table at his sister store in Toronto, marked down to one third of the original price. He would not make any commission on this item, had gone to considerable trouble to find it and had taken the liberty of securing it and having it sent over for me. I have since dedicated all of my purchases to Derik Simpson, who has made a long series of profound service gestures on my behalf. *Great service builds a platform for long-term trust, permanent high-margin purchasing and frequent good referrals. Great service providers suspend their self-interest to do the things that really touch their clients, and their clients respond with their loyalty and evangelism.*

The Answer in the Question   8
Finding Out What Works for Each Entrepreneur

In starting my professional career as a design consultant, I had mistaken the belief that I had to have all the answers to any questions my clients might pose. One of my first projects was working with a client in the aircraft repair business. The president of the company commissioned us to make a new container to carry food onto the airplanes. I was presenting aesthetic concepts for the containers when the client asked a question relating to our proposed treatment of an aluminum detail. I was embarrassed by having no clue to the answer to his question. "I don't have a clue" didn't seem like the way to go, so I bluffed my way through a response, as only a really insecure kid could. For some reason, it did not occur to me that this client, who had worked for years with every imaginable kind of aluminum in every imaginable way, would be able to catch me in such an obvious lie. He was very polite in reminding me of his knowledge in the area, and he let me off without the requisite thrashing. As it turned out, all I needed to to do was say, "I do not know, but I know where to find out."

I learned a subtler version of this lesson as a neophyte seminar leader. Seminars work better when they are done heuristically, that is, when the facilitator leads participants to their own answers. Unfortunately for me, I like being right and spent a lot of time giving people their answers and making them wrong when they offered their own insight as a defense to my preaching. I earned the unfortunate moniker "the sage on a stage", to reflect this perhaps charming but certainly ineffective part of my personality.

On one particular occasion, I was working with a dentist who had spoken often about intimacy in his practice but who was struggling to see that it was the core of his business: "helping people get close", as he would later articulate. At one moment in the seminar I smugly said, "Bill, I will tell you who you are: you are about intimacy!" Enamored by my own supposed brilliance, I failed to notice his deflated look. Later he gave me the piece of feedback that, while he agreed with me, he did not appreciate me stealing a moment of insight from him. Still not quite grasping the whole arrogance thing, I simply replied, "Well, Bill, that's the thing about us self-righteous people...we are right most of the time." It seems entrepreneurs have their own answers. My job, I have found out, which is far easier to do than to grasp sometimes, is to ask really good questions. I do not see myself getting paid for answers anymore. I am getting paid for questions.

Good questions open up a world of possibility. My favourites draw out the best opportunities for creating new value. What are you so passionate about you would do for free? What is your unique contribution? What sets you apart from every other lawyer, accountant, financial planner or architect in your market? Where are you going? What do you most want to create? What is working? What is not? What is your greatest challenge? What stresses you? What are the three most important commitments you have to keep in the next two weeks? Ninety days? Three years? For the rest of your life? What does good support look like to you? Who are your people? What kind of people do you like best? What qualities do your favourite people possess? What do your people require from you? What is most important to you? Given that you are not currently dead, what ideals are you prepared to fight for? What is your legacy going to be? What were you born to do? What are your strongest beliefs about life? Who are you? Why are you here? *The best questions inspire a deep personal introspection about what matters most in life and invoke powerful insights buried under the surface of the urgent daily grind.*

The integrative health practice of iridology is a healing practice that uses clues from the iris of the eye to glean insights about what is going on in the patient's life. Expressions such as "the eyes have it" or "that certain look in the eye" also connote the allure of the eye and what is going on behind it. Looking people in the eye is a sign of respect, and the eye reflects people's authority and their confidence in what they see. The eye is the source of vision.

In the entrepreneurial context, vision represents the future path of a venture. It is at once a reflection of the opportunities afforded by the commercial environment and the deep creative yearnings held tightly within the entrepreneurs. The vision represents the calling and the venture is the formal ordaining of an entrepreneur on a lifelong journey of enterprise, contribution and service. To an entrepreneur a meaningful business that represents an important calling feels like home. It is the way of life in which we spend all of our days in passionate pursuit.

The spiritual journey and the struggle of awakening to the call of higher purpose is the process of waking from what Saint John of the Cross called "the dark night of the soul." It is for people the dawning of light in their lives – a consciousness illuminating a more purposeful and meaningful existence. Such light may be a challenge to see. For a long time, the U2 song, "I still haven't found what I'm looking for" was a harsh, though beautiful reminder that I had not really found my true calling. I was seeking my true nature, my path and my purpose. It was, however, evading me.

As young men, my friend Karl and I stood at the same apparent crossroads. He chose to become a mountain guide, and I chose to explore entrepreneurship, engineering and design school. Karl quickly became a very adept and successful guide, one of the youngest and fastest people to gain full credentials.

My friends and I once hired Karl to teach us some advanced mountain techniques. We got up early, one late Autumn morning, stumbled out onto a glacier and the performance began. That day was overcast and blustery. Cold and snow were whipping our freezing faces. We sat, shivering and sniveling, as Karl worked to set up the scenarios we were going to learn. It was then I caught that certain look in his eye. It was as if this place was his stage and he was giving his best performance. Despite our misery and the brutal, inhospitable conditions, Karl was happy to his bones and completely at home. At that moment, I knew I had not found my own stage, the place where I was completely at home, doing what I was meant to do. I lacked that look.

The following summer, I found myself 20 feet from Colin James, playing on-stage at a free outdoor concert. At one point, he was ripping through some soulful blues riff and I caught that same look in his eye. I can still see it frozen in my mind's eye. It's the look that someone has when they do not want to be anywhere else, doing anything else. They are at home in the moment. And at that moment I found my own calling: to help entrepreneurs find theirs.

I believe that everyone has a calling, a higher purpose, a reason for being. When we seek it, we experience flow, inner peace, Nirvana and all the beauty and bounty of life's gift for us. For some, the search is for something outside of themselves. I had mine all the time. I just did not look inside for it. The passionate path is ultimately an inner journey that finds its way out into the world of possibility and creation: the calling comes from within, not without. Consciousness is the inner light illuminating the dark night of future potential. *A person who has found home on the stage of their life is a bright light for others to see their own.*

Entrepreneurial Styles   **10**

Finding a Good Way as an Entrepreneur

The psychologist Carl Gustav Jung wrote a seminal work on personality styles. He proposed four personality "energies" that manifest in different proportions in different people: director, observer, inspirer and supporter. Jung's energy topology also implies different approaches to entrepreneurship. Ed McMullan and Wayne Long in their book *Developing New Ventures*, assessed the historical writings of the American economist Joseph Schumpeter, along with European writers from the late 18th and 19th centuries such as Jean-Baptiste Say, Richard Cantillon and Abbe Nicolas Baudeau. Their work suggests a wide definition of entrepreneurial character and identifies the primary archetypes and valences of the entrepreneur: as creative innovator, as risk-taker and promoter, as enterprising manager and undertaker, as value creator and marshaler of productive resources.

In my topology, an entrepreneurial style reflects the orientation a person has along two dimensions. The first dimension reflects field orientation: introverts are introspective and oriented towards internal capabilities and resources; extroverts are oriented towards customers, competitors and the external business environment. The second dimension reflects structural orientation: unstructured people are oriented to vision and starting and structured people are oriented to process and finishing. Depending on these orientations, entrepreneurs have a primary mode of innovation, as promoter, capitalist, designer or facilitator.

Unstructured extroverts are "promoters" who innovate by inspiring people to become excited and buy into the venture. With naturally strong presentation skills, promoters attract and enroll customers, staff and investors. Excited by "world changing" concepts, promoters are prepared to take risks but can be superficial and image-conscious, often stumbling over or avoiding completion and details, while fearing commitment and loss of freedom. Promoters are great evangelists.

Structured extroverts are "facilitators" who innovate by undertaking the rollout of the venture and by making progress easier and faster. With naturally strong people skills, facilitators find and nurture the genuine value in any relationship. Facilitators are compassionate people, but they can get stuck in "rescue missions" and in not taking care of themselves, fearing other's judgment that they are selfish or unworthy. Facilitators are great supporters.

Structured introverts are "designers" who innovate by inventing brilliant and novel systems and structures. With naturally strong product and production skills, designers create elegant solutions to complex problems. Designers are careful and logical thinkers, but with an affinity for office supplies and a fear of being wrong they can get stuck in "analysis paralysis", wallowing in details to the expense of the big picture. Designers are great prototypers.

Unstructured introverts are "capitalists" who innovate by marshaling and increasing the value of resources in the venture: time, people, money and ideas. With naturally strong skills in task execution, capitalists drive the venture forward towards powerful results. Capitalists are highly committed and quick decision-makers, but they can be judgmental and lack sensitivity, getting stuck in the need to be right while mistrusting their teammates. Capitalists are great achievers.

Each entrepreneurial style represents a different and equally valuable approach to innovation, leadership and venture creation. While we may have some capacity to shift from style to style as needed, we all tend to default to our primary style under stress. *Each of us needs some combination of teamwork, partnership or exquisite self-care and mastery to balance the different energies that must flow into the productive building and operation of our ventures.*

Back in the days of fur-lined toilet seats and rhinestone-covered bathroom accessories, the environmental designer, historian and theorist Victor Papanek wrote a scathing critique of the industrial design profession. He suggested that the profession of product design was second only to the advertising business in its utter lack of moral virtue. His seditious comments were nonetheless accurate: thirty years ago marketing was about convincing people to buy things they didn't need, with money they didn't have, to impress people who didn't care. He may have been impressed with how the marketing and product design professions have altered their orientation to more substantive and satisfying value creating exercises. Thirty years ago, marketers were genuinely in business to trick people into buying their often inferior goods. Manufacturers appreciated whatever superficial cosmetic flourishes designers could add to slick-up the offering and lure the masses.

Today, buyers seek authenticity. Consumers are now viewing products and services as more than technical objects. "The faceless masses" now want to identify with the people who make what they buy and use and they are searching for something more spiritual.

Consider the snowboard market. During the first winter Olympics that included the sport, and just after Canada won a gold medal for the first ever snowboard event, there was a huge scandal over tests that revealed that the victorious boarder had perhaps smoked a "doobie" the day before. I have no problem with Marijuana use, as I doubt its power as a sport-enhancing drug, but I do recall thinking that snowboarders are sure different from skiers. No skier has been caught with pot that I recall. Boarders also use different gear, go outside for different reasons, use different language and certainly dress in very different clothing.

Snowboarders seem rebellious to me. Perhaps it comes from their skateboarding and surfing roots. Perhaps it is comes from their Generation Y and Internet ranks and their dislike for tradition and the boomer generation that went before them. Whatever the source is of their more radical approach to the slopes, it often comes with a distaste for anything to do with skiing and the traditional skiing business. There is a saying that "people convert to snowboarding but not the other way around." Snowboarders are definitely not skiers.

In the last decade, the big news in the winter sports world was the entry of the snowboarding contingent, who have shaken up the industry and added some much needed interest and money to the slopes and to the stores. This should have been good news for suppliers in the outdoor industry. It should have been good for the ski business. However, it was not good news all around.

Despite the great snow conditions during many years in the recent past, and despite the entry of the boarders, it has not been good for the many people who make and sell ski equipment and clothing. Many local suppliers, skiwear retailers and even the largest outerwear manufacturers have suffered some downturns in their businesses. Many ski suppliers have been trying to serve the new market, with gear designed for them, but many authenticity-suspicious boarders are not buying it.

They are buying gear designed by boarders for boarders, from new startups that are themselves bucking the inertia of the establishment and bringing in new ideas and concepts and a new movement. It is not that gear offered by the traditional ski companies is inferior for any technical reason. Snowboarders simply identify more with the "spirit" of these new suppliers: "They are us, and we are them." *Authenticity reflects the meaningful connection customers have with a company that is more important than the basic technical quality of its products.*

Elevating the Conversation   12
Expressing the True Identity of a Business

The American philosopher-economist Thorstein Bunde Veblen coined the term "conspicuous consumption" to capture his observations about the relationship between people and the goods they buy. The term denotes the tendency of newly-monied people, his so called "leisure class", to spend and consume in such a way that loudly announces their newly-acquired status in the social strata: "I shop, therefore I am", as one bumper sticker neatly summed up Yuppie consumerism. In this context, a company's brand symbolizes its prestige and is coveted for this reason alone, hence the pejorative label of being "brand-conscious."

In the 1980s, such brand-consciousness may have truly overshadowed any of the genuine value hidden inside the company and its products. Companies became vacuous social symbols, and it did not take long for many brands to end up at Wal-Mart and other low-margin commodity peddlers, where ultimately the decision became one of price. Many companies, Gucci being one famous example, lost their cache – and cash; and some companies, like Pierre Cardin, never recovered.

Despite the residue of ill-will, we can rework the notion of a brand to reflect the trend towards more meaningful life and experience. A brand becomes more than a pecuniary symbol of prestige. It becomes a statement of identity – a reflection of the values housed at the core of the business. A good brand establishes greater integrity by infusing core values into the fabric of the business, into every detail and deed. Core values represent what founders hold to be most important, what they stand for and what they are striving to create.

The buyer-domain of an enterprise is its brand: how potential customers come to identify with the company by appreciating its values. The brand is the story behind a company's creation; its verbal, written and visual language; its character and everything it honestly presents to its customers. People ultimately buy on value. If we elevate the marketing conversation from one of "value for money", which attracts price-shoppers, to one of "authentic core values", we are more likely to attract permanent high-margin customers. Such a conversation reflects the world view of the company – what it ultimately exists to create – and is more spiritual than technical. The world view speaks to the highest and best aspirations of the company founders and is more inspiring to clients than the logistics of a purchase. The best clients do not buy on price or on features. They do not buy on technology. They buy on the basis of their identification with the company's world view, on their emotional connection to the company. And when they buy-in, they tend to stay bound.

California-based Patagonia makes clothing for the outdoors – two of my passions. When I started ice climbing, the classic book on the subject was authored by the same man who created Patagonia – Yvon Chouinard. The book poetically captured his philosophy of life, relating to the satisfaction of simple living and our reintegration with nature. Resonating deeply with this concept, I then found that the same thinking had found its way into the design of his company's garments. I have spent generously on his offerings not just for their prestige but because of a spiritual connection with him. His values are transparent throughout the enterprise and have created a strong base of long-term residual income from repeat business, enduring customer goodwill and respect for the integrity of the company by all the people who care for it. *The best marketing is not a description of product features and technology that no one will care about in four business quarters; the best marketing engages people in a meaningful conversation about what everyone cares most about, has cared most about and will care most about.*

On Growing a Spine   13
Taking a Stand for What is Most Important

One of my childhood friends, Peter Morris, worked in the product development business for some time and we did a number of challenging projects together. I was always amazed by his ability to marshal subcontractors to a client's cause and protect his suppliers from their vagaries and whims. He was always a bold champion for his team and stood tall for the rights of all the people he had enrolled to build the product. Of all the things I appreciate about Peter is his well-developed backbone. I sometimes saw Peter's role as helping a fledgling startup venture develop their own. New ventures are a character-building enterprise. Spineless ventures buckle and fold.

I have always been impressed by the sight of someone taking a stand for something they hold as important, asserting their point of view in defiance of the critics. This act of defiance is the essential act of enterprise and innovation and one of the most important jobs for the lead entrepreneur. Design school gave us the opportunity to strengthen our characters through the rite of passage known as the design critique. These sometimes punishing experiences were formal presentation and review sessions in front of peers and teachers. Crits taught aspiring designers to separate themselves from their creative product and to defend the decisions they made about why this detail should be that way and why that detail should be the other. No one survived five years of design school without developing a more rigourous professional character. The spineless designers buckled and folded.

As any member of the vertebrate family is conceived and grows, the development of the spine is its defining characteristic. From the moment of conception, the nascent embryo begins to take on the form of a central nervous system, culminating in the structure of a fully developed spine. The spine establishes the basic framework on which all other systems ultimately take hold. The spinal cord is among the first major manifestations of the codes held in the DNA.

In the creation of a startup, the embryonic venture begins with a set of codes not unlike organic DNA. This code is the value-set held by the founders of the company. Core values may well be more than just a commercial analog. As the complex biological instruction set drives the development of an organic body, its cultural equivalent drives the corporate body.

As we all mature, through countless experiences and brushes with other humans, we all learn what is most important to us. Our core values are those concepts and principles that we hold dear, that define our personal sense of integrity. When we think and act according to this value set, we are in alignment with our values and we could say that the products of our creative endeavours possess that most precious quality of integrity.

Our core values are those things that through time have pulled us with such strength that we have learned not to compromise on them. When we breach a core value, we feel the irritation, stress and pain as if it were a deep moral offense and violation. Deeds, words and objects of creation missing a clear root in our value systems lack the integrity essential to our feeling of deep fulfillment. Anything built from the stuff of our core values is meaningful. Anything else lacks the foundational character that makes any creative product seem significant and worthwhile. The good brands, cultures, teams, products and capital structures we design reflect a set of values we share with the people who contact them. They are good in the moral sense. *The source of all joy and stress lies in the creation or destruction of core values, what is most important to us, what we stand for and what drives us forward in our entrepreneurial pursuits.*

Speaking with Soul   14
Making the Long Journey to the Voice Within

A former standup comic named Dan Gascon made the painful and ultimately successful journey from an almost abusive "the joke is on you" style to developing a compassionate and respectful program called *Humour for Your Health*. Dan's original comedy styling was an adoption of the caustic and sarcastic approach that was the standard when he started in the business. Deep down though it was Dan that felt the sting every time he made someone else the brunt of his joke. Then he found his real sense of humour. Dan defines humour as "letting other people see your joy." Authentic humour means casting off false images of other peoples' style and approach and dis-covering our own joy, our own voice. I have met other people who are learning standup and the lesson is always the same. It is not until people connect with their joy that they see the irony and humour in life. This is the dialogue with our real selves.

The same seems to be true of all creative pursuits: the arts, public speaking and even the creation of an enterprise. When we listen to our inner voice and not the outer voice of a false public we access an abundant creative source.

Writing has been a long and interesting process of finding myself. As a child, I neither wrote nor read much and had a weak command of vocabulary, grammar and syntax as a result. In high school, I barely passed English class: I had the lowest mark possible while still passing. To get into University, I had to actually repeat high school English and barely passed the second time. Then I failed the University entrance exam – a written essay – twice. There was something about taking a point of view and building an argument in writing that always seemed out of my grasp. So I was then forced to take a first year English class, which I barely passed. In Engineering School, the linear scientific method preempted any opportunity at creative pursuits. I took a technical writing course, which I barely passed. In my first month of Graduate School, I wrote a paper so poorly that it prompted the Professor to write a letter to the Dean of the Faculty, stating, "Keith's writing is so poor, I doubt that he has the intellectual ability to graduate." This was a wake-up call that prompted my interest in language and, in particular, the Thesaurus. I discovered grandiose, polysyllabic words to obfuscate my thoughts. I eventually learned to read and write technically well and wrote a thesis, but my writing remained ethereal and obtuse. (I used lots of words like obfuscate, ethereal and obtuse.)

Years later, I started writing professionally when I made an agreement with Jay Levinson to co-write a book. Jay is a very well-known and best-selling business author who has a strong literary agent and a strong presence with New York publishers: his support would expedite my book's publishing. The first task was to write a book proposal for the literary agent, Mike Larsen, a man who knows his business very well. After writing and presenting at least six very weak proposals to Mike, I was successful at alienating him, which prompted his advice: "You might want to consider hiring a writer." Even Jay who was a committed mentor by then commented, "I prefer writing that is clear and concise; yours is neither." Clearly I had lots of work to do.

For me writing is a joyful experience, and I see the humour in my journey. I can spend hours, in complete bliss, pursuing the elusive moment of elegant prose. This is my joy. Finally, after twenty years, I have found my own voice. I have cast off the images of what "good writing" is and who "good writers" are. I have made cautious friends with the English language. *Authentic self-expression is a lifelong journey, made humble by the awesome power of the creative source and joyful by the simple grace of well-chosen words.*

A Triumph of Style and Substance   15
Pursuing the Integrity of Higher Values and Visions

I bought my first Apple Macintosh computer in 1988. It had a screen the size of a postcard, and I had to pay extra for a hard drive. It had 1 megabyte of RAM and cost $2800. That was a big deal. Then I paid $7800 for my first workstation. I bought my first PowerBook laptop for $5000 and more workstations and laptops, all of which were hundreds of times slower than the laptop from which these words flowed. Compared to what I could have paid for PCs, I have invested a large premium in the products of Apple Computer, the vision of Steve Jobs and a platform of values I felt worthy of my support. I bought these computers from Apple because Apple was different. It represented a counterpoint to the imperialism of Wintel, the powerful alliance between Microsoft and Intel. To me this is a revolution, and the higher prices I pay are a contribution to a viable alternative to ubiquity.

The Macintosh is not just a product, it is a movement. On the rear cover of a Time magazine was an ad featuring a simple image of Mahatma Gandhi with an Apple logo and the mantra: "Think Different." I have seen other such images of great innovators like Einstein and Edison, all with the same treatment. The company remains an important phenomenon despite many bouts of fiscal difficulty and the dark period between Jobs' tenures, when the various CEOs appeared to have had no clue about what the company meant to its customers and only offered poorly-designed and poorly-built PC-like junk. It has made impressive forays into the consumer market place, creating a wealth of loyal patrons and an impressive recovery from near-bankruptcy. Indeed, "Mac people" are not just enthusiastic, we represent our own unique demographic – a community of creative people loyal to the platform and revolution. And technology alone does not explain why people rally behind the company with such passion. What founder, and "iCEO", Steve Jobs stands for does.

One of the most interesting things about the new Apple is that its CEO did not really get paid to come back. Despite some bonuses, his salary in cash and stock was $1 the year he returned. Since reclaiming the company, he has rebuilt it from the ground up, doubling the value of the company, while also doubling the value of Pixar, his other company. He did not appear to rejoin Apple for the money. He rejoined Apple because he wanted to recreate the company. This is his passion. Creativity first, even rebellious creativity, seems to be at the core of Apple. And its founder is walking the talk.

What matters to Jobs and Apple is good design – "the fundamental soul of a man-made creation that ends up expressing itself in successive outer layers of the product or service." Apple hardware and software are legendary for their aesthetics and that could easily be written off as superficial style. But they are also famous for being easy to use and easy to integrate into a person's life. This reflects Jobs' fastidious commitment to the user experience and ground-up creativity. That is substance and reflects the life purpose of the founder. Apple customers get both style and substance.

This is not merely about branding, but the deeper process of entrepreneurs creating meaning for their customers by expressing who they are. It is about improving the quality of life for people and rising above the commodity.

All entrepreneurs can integrate a deeper experience into the purchase and use of their services and products by taking a stand for what they really believe in and walking their talk. *Doing business in ways that reflect the life purpose and core values of people that work in and on an enterprise is more attractive and more deeply satisfying to its customers than the commodities it makes and sells.*

I grew up in an enterprising household, with parents that had careers that started in the 1950s. Both my mother and father had ventures of their own and it was open for my brother and I to pursue whatever enterprises we wanted. Despite the freedom they gave us, both of our parents were commanding authority figures in our lives. As entrepreneurs, steeped in the management practices of the day, my parents ran their affairs with a high degree of command and control – a predominant feature of how most corporations were and still run.

Like many men of my generation, I had a difficult relationship with my father at times. He was larger than life to me, with a powerful command of the English language, an easy way with people and an adventurous spirit. Men of his generation, born early in the last century, did not develop an overabundance of intimacy skills. It was simply not a priority and it was certainly not viewed as manly to get close to other men. So I did not really get to know my dad and I certainly did not understand why he did what he did. He was just this imposing figure that invaded my space from time to time. Sometimes I preferred his angry outbursts over the longer bouts of indifference that were free of any emotion at all. In my mid-twenties, I decided to distance myself from him. I cannot even remember where my anger came from. I just know at that time, I saw no purpose to fatherhood.

This, of course, changed with the arrival of my son, when I realized I was beginning to become what I resented in my own father, or worse, becoming so much the opposite of my dad that I disavowed the important values and the virtues he had passed on, like the importance of family and personal freedom.

At about this time, I began my personal growth journey. Looking inside for the first time, I saw my own weaknesses with intimacy, and my own high need for control. But I also figured out what I wanted from life, what was important to me. I began to put aside the notions, visions and ideas I had acquired from the outside world, from my parents, from culture at large, and began the arduous task of building my life and my business from the inside out. This was the moment I began to be accountable for myself, the moment I started my journey of authenticity.

I remember blaming my father. I do not remember what I thought was his fault, but I do remember attributing much of my misery to him. I judged him for his weaknesses and the things he did wrong, and then I blamed him for teaching me the same ways. It was not until I realized that I had acquired some of his strengths and the things he did well that I started to get the idea. There is a circle that completes itself from the father to the son to the grandson. At some point in all of our lives, there is the opportunity to live for ourselves, while taking our place in the generational sequence. This moment is a moment of acceptance, of taking ownership over our own values and visions.

There is ample empirical evidence and a mass of anecdotes about how our parents influence us in both positive and negative aspects. Whether it comes from genetic heritage or early childhood socialization, our parents pass on the good and bad parts of themselves. And we do the same for our children. Denying this fact is a waste of time. I now imagine that I have a place inside of me where I store all of the good things I have to offer. Sometimes I keep these things locked up, and I become my own oppressor. I have come to appreciate that the lock I keep on this box of virtues is made up of all the negative judgments I have about my parents and myself. My own vices are guarding my own virtues. The key is to take ownership over my shadow side. *As we come to accept our own faults and flaws, and those of the people around us, we release more of our value into the world.*

Taking Ownership Over Customer Expectations

I was passing, once, through a high-end store in Vancouver, when I saw a beautiful pair of shoes that reminded me of the old English-style brogues my dad used to have with the dimpled leather. I felt compelled to purchase them. Since the store had a sister store in Calgary, I chose to bypass the provincial sales tax and buy them at home. The person who took my order turned out to be the manager of the men's shoe department. It was a very brief exchange of the product code I had for a swipe of my bank card. I was in and out in under two minutes. Two weeks later, I whisked in to pick up the shoes that were waiting for me at the counter. The manager was assisting another client, gave me a friendly nod, and I was off.

Two years later, tragedy struck. The seam on one of the shoes began to pull apart. Unhappy at this development, given the price I had paid for a reputable brand from a reputable store, I prepared for the inevitable battle between the big mean exploitive store and the hapless retail victim.

As I rolled down the escalator, into the habitat of the shoe department manager, I could feel the blood flowing into my face, as I prepared for the fight. The manager saw me coming as I descended into the shoe area. I braced for the conflict, rehearsing in my mind the speech I had prepared to press my rights and rectify this grave retail injustice. I approached the counter and before I could launch my first sortie, he said, "Hello Mr. Hanna, do you have a problem with your Ferragamos? Let me have a look. We have the best shoe guy in town; I can get these fixed up for you no charge. Is tomorrow OK for you?" All I could choke out was, "OK", and "thank you." This fellow, who had only met me briefly years before, remembered my name and took immediate ownership of the problem. This kind gesture completely avoided the fault and blame exercise and went straight to surpassing my expectations.   He took accountability and vapourized the problem.

In the famous and mythical restaurant service study, researchers tracked the results of various service outcomes and scenarios regarding goodwill. In scenario one, a patron had an error-free experience and typically told a few people, "check out that restaurant." In scenario two, the patron had a poor service experience that wait staff failed to correct. The patron left unsatisfied and the birth of a powerful new cautionary tale occurred: "never go to that place." This one traveled like a virus. In the third scenario, an error occurred, the staff corrected the temporary dissatisfaction and the restaurant became a hero. Patrons in this case referred more people to a restaurant that had corrected an error than if the service had been perfect in the first place.

It seems that good service is inconspicuous. It also seems that during the service episode while the client is just "dissatisfied" it is still possible to satisfy their expectations. Once they leave "unsatisfied", this situation becomes unrecoverable, and they become ill-will generators. Thus any good service system creates a clear interface for lucid client feedback, so servers can adjust their experience in realtime, rather than find out after the fact and after it is too late.

Customers are unhappy only when some service contact fails to meet an expectation. Many expectations are of course the unconscious, unstated kind, which surface quickly whenever it is time to pay. It is obviously not practical to perfectly anticipate all expectation. It might be better to respond well to errors that have happened. Accountability for error is not about blaming others or ourselves for causing the problem but accepting ownership of the situation. *We are accountable for all errors for which we personally pay a price, not because we or someone else is to blame but simply because our clients expected more from us.*

Standing on Solid Ground

Building Strong Cultures that Work

Academic studies of entrepreneurs over the years have revealed an interesting number of observations about the entrepreneurial psyche. Among these are that entrepreneurs have high needs for power and control; for freedom, independence and excellence; for creativity, challenge and expression and for attention, excitement and recognition. When entrepreneurs get these needs met constructively, their companies thrive.

A strong culture promotes constructive need satisfaction. Deeply set in the minds of every entrepreneur are strong convictions about the way things ought to be. Conviction is grounded in strongly held beliefs which can manifest in both powerfully negative and positive ways. Such beliefs constitute the cultures of the organizations we create and lead. Culture is like the ground everyone stands on. It can be solid or shaky. Culture, in this sense, is the net effect of all beliefs held by members of the team. A solid culture that works contains a predominance of positive and affirmative convictions that inspire the creativity of all the people in a company.

A shaky culture that does not work becomes a cult of limiting, negative beliefs that weigh down the spirit of the enterprise and lead ultimately to self-defeating, destructive behaviours. A cult is a limiting belief system that is ultimately destructive. Cults need not be religious perversions. They exist everywhere in the systems we build. Three such cults create shaky ground: the cult of performance, the cult of perfection and the cult of personality.

The cult of performance is a perversion of the drive towards achievement and a high need for challenge. The limiting belief in this cult is "everything has to be hard." This belief has many connotations: "good things take time" or "if something is easy, it can't possibly be good." The problem with these beliefs is that it is quite easy to invent artificial challenges and make things more complicated and time-consuming than they really are, so we can experience the thrill of the win. By letting simple tasks remain simple, we focus on more productive challenges, like solving more challenging customer problems.

The cult of perfection is a perversion of the drive towards control and a high need to be right. The limiting belief in this cult is "it has to look a certain way." This is a self-righteous position that ignores input from employees or clients. Idealistic entrepreneurs often create a puristic fantasy of the world, resulting in unattainable standards. This perpetuates thoughts that "no one and nothing is ever good enough", "we are not worthy" or "there is not enough to go around." It is from this place that the company's self-esteem erodes, leading to destructive behaviours like underbidding, over promising and under delivering. A more compassionate view creates more realistic approaches and a focus on excellence rather than a focus on perfection.

The cult of personality is a perversion of the drive towards recognition, acceptance and a high need to be liked and validated. This is the heroic, Marlborough Man part of an entrepreneur that says, "I can do everything myself." This drive also shows up as, "if I accept help, I am weak" or even worse, "I cannot trust people to do the job right." So no one ever learns to work together or to delegate, and all synergy and accountability are lost. A more creative approach is a deep respect for the contributions of everyone, which leads to everyone sharing and capitalizing on each other's value.

There is an affirmative belief for every limiting one. *Solid ground is a strong set of affirmative beliefs that supports everyone on the team to find productive outlets for the fulfillment of their driving needs.*

Writing and Telling the Stories that Tell Us Who We Are

The great American mythologist Joseph Campbell told of how ancient peoples stored and transmitted their knowledge from generation to generation. Important elements of tribal history, ethics and politics and the complicated system of survival techniques, tools and technology found their way into a complex web of stories carefully guarded by the elders of the tribe. These stories are not like the detailed and procedural operating manuals gathering dust on the shelves of most companies today. They were richly coloured illustrations of sophisticated operating principles and value systems that guided the young people of the group in finding their way and place in the group. The stories contained the entire culture of a social group, and certain clan members had the sacred task of memorizing the stories word for word, so that they could be passed on word for word to successors.

Beaverton-based, Nike is among the first of the great global companies to introduce corporate mythology. Nike may be a great deal more sophisticated than a typical primitive tribe, but every new employee still gets initiated into the Nike lore: the early days around the track in Oregon, Steve Prefontaine, the waffle sole, the air bags, Air Jordon, the myth of the goddess of victory and the slogan, "Just do it." Instead of memorizing a pedantic manual of rules and corporate happy-speak, the new initiates receive a rite of passage into a long corporate history.

Myths teach us who we are in the grander context of an expanding cosmos. A corporate mythology is a more interesting kind of employee manual for communicating the rules and standards of conduct for any company. Myths and stories seem to capture the nuance of a concept, principle or precept in a way that a more flaccid procedural description cannot. First, the language is more human. Manuals tend to read like scientific lab experiments from high school. Second, a story has a moral, and the moral has an emotional framework around it that gives it fuller affect. Stories are experiential, flexible and colourful. Procedures are black and white, strict and lifeless.

My mother wrote the mythology of the company she recently retired from. As the chief sales officer of a professional apartment hotel, catering to upscale professionals visiting the city for prolonged periods of time, she held a prominent place in the company and the relationships between the company, its staff and its customers. Like any business there were rules and standards that guests and employees needed to respect in order to preserve a beneficial experience for everyone.

One of these rules was the "no pet rule." Pets are annoying to other guests and often leave unpleasant messes. So, pets were not welcome. Unfortunately, many guests traveling to the city for extended work assignments often brought their families with them. Within the extended families were dogs and cats to which the families had strong emotional connections. Often guests resisted the "no pet rule" and tried many creative tactics to prey on the weaknesses of staff. To make matters worse, the retired owner of the business, who resided on the premises, kept his own dog on site in plain view of the other guests. My mother learned effective responses to objections to this policy. It was not enough to teach the staff that there are to be no pets allowed. My mother wrote a series of stories depicting how she had effectively handled these incidents as well as other subtleties of the operations of the business. Like a tribal elder, she wrote and passed on the mythology to her successors, leaving the best part of herself behind, past her retirement. *Myths and stories can be more effective than procedure manuals in teaching new staff about the rich patina and deep heritage of valuable learning residing in the culture of the enterprise.*

Making an Emotional Choice

Of all the things I have done, there are few that have been as uncomfortable as speaking in public. One fear I have is the fear of being humiliated and laid bare in front of a mob of unfriendly strangers bent on my destruction. The stage seems as good a place as any for this. This fear has operated in the background, frequently undermining my forward progress. I had been avoiding the book publishing thing for years precisely because I would need to go out in public and speak for it. At some moment I chose to face this fear and commit to publishing this book. That commitment was an emotional choice, a choice to overcome a fear and move outside of my comfort zone.

It turns out that public speaking is quite fulfilling. I get my need for acknowledgment met as I am up there speaking about some topic I care about and assisting an audience in acknowledging the importance of the topic in their own lives. The more people that appear to "get it", the happier I am.

It also turns out that I am largely in control of whether people understand and appreciate my point of view. This has to do with how I deal with criticism, the event that triggers my fear of humiliation. If I am not in a good space to hear someone's feedback, I can easily hear it as an invalidation. If I am in a good space I respond well even to negative feedback.

I once participated in a panel discussion on the topic of viral marketing. My role was to lay out the history and main conceptual framework underlying the topic. At the end of the panel, we answered questions from the audience. The first few were quite fun, and I enjoyed the challenge of responding to each. Then, a gentleman at the back asked a very direct and seemingly confrontative question: "This just seems like marketing 101 all over to me; how is it different?" I typically see such a comment either as a great gift to the conversation and the opportunity to learn something new or I dismiss the comment thinking, "He is trying to embarrass me in front of everyone." Fortunately, I saw the opportunity in his question and thought "What a great question."

I had always thought that much of the New Economy banter was just reworked, or relanguaged, Old Economy ideas and concepts. I acknowledged his question, thought carefully of my answer and articulated a response that he liked so much he became a client. He told me after that he felt well acknowledged for raising an important issue that led to the audience coming to appreciate a subtle distinction between new and old marketing. It seems funny that I might have dismissed him.

As part of my training for the stage, I took a three month leadership program that used public speaking to help us draw out our assets and overcome our liabilities. During the reviews of my first videotaped presentations, I was ready to vomit at my first sight of me in "dismissive preacher" mode. I had never realized what an arrogant, know-it-all I was. Preaching and making people wrong were ways in which I got my acknowledgment need met at someone's expense. Ironically, people seem to love to attack arrogant, self-righteous people.

I have since learned to be more vulnerable, humble and astute on stage by taking the position that everyone has a special contribution to make. I have never been attacked in this mode of being, because I am open to the needs of the audience and can articulate meaningful concepts and ideas. "Astute articulating" works better than "dismissive preaching." From this place of strength, I see the constructive feedback that lies in every apparent or anticipated "criticism." *When we reframe threatening situations, we overcome the fear that prevents us from exploiting important opportunities to get our needs met constructively, in the service of others.*

My first professional speaking engagement was opening for Jay Levinson, a seasoned speaker and the best selling author of the Guerrilla Marketing Series. As a neophyte speaker, I was anxious about my performance, and he had kind words to help me take the stage with more confidence. While waiting in the wings to be introduced, Jay told me of his first speaking engagement after becoming a writer of note. He was himself waiting in the wings to be introduced to the hundreds of people gathered. He listened to the introduction, strangely dis-associated from the event. On cue, he mounted the stage, placed his hands at the side of the podium, looked out at the sea of people gathered in front of him and realized that the room was dead silent. It was a moment of anticipation. All eyes were on him. He could have heard the proverbial pin drop. There was only one person who was going to fill that room with sound that day. This was the sobering moment of accountability: the cold realization that no one else was going to save him or do it for him.

Every once and a while, I go ice climbing by myself. In some remote alpine area, miles away from another person, hundreds of feet off the deck with no rope and only my tools and technique to keep the ground at bay, the notion of accountability has no ambiguity. I fall, I die. It is actually pretty simple and pretty clear: I pay the price for the choice that led to the moment of culpability.

While it may be thrilling to solo an ice climb or business venture, it is nice to have the company of other people to make the journey more fun and surely safer. The difficulty with accountability and its sister notion of responsibility is the complication of adding other people to the enterprise. It can be like the day I arrived at an ice climb with someone I did not know well only to find that neither of us had brought the rope: "I thought you brought the rope"..."No, I thought you did."

In business settings, where there is usually no real death threat to focus the participants, it is much easier to confuse accountability and responsibility. In traditional teams, with a group of followers and a leader, the leader has legitimate authority to command the team. Historically, large climbing expeditions to far off Himalayan peaks utilized this military system of command and control. The great management theorist Peter Drucker pointed out that this method of organization is not unlike an orchestra, with an autocratic conductor commanding the players according to a fixed score. In climbing expeditions, musical troupes and entrepreneurial ventures, this type of arrangement is too inflexible and too slow to be fulfilling for the participants and to be responsive to a rapidly changing creative environment.

The idea of the team has changed considerably. Large, siege-style climbing expeditions have given way to smaller and more nimble alpine-ascent teams, moving confidently over changing terrain, with changing weather. Likewise, large corporate bureaucracies have given way to more nimble and powerful teams of enterprising people. These ventures compete effectively in a chaotic environment of vicious competition, uneducated clients and expanding technology by improvising an unending stream of new approaches and solutions. This is how a jazz quartet works. There is no score. There is mutual respect. Everyone on the team rises on the stage to play their part when needed. Each player is at once an autonomous creative entity and part of an unfolding synergy.

True accountability and power occur when each of us takes ownership over a result, instead of waiting to be told. *Systems of single-source accountability make it very clear to everyone on a team who owns a result and, therefore, who has the ultimate power to decide how that result will come to be.*

Changing the Mental Programs that Drive Results

My wife and I have been weight training for over a year. Watching her lift has been an exercise in humility, as she regularly lifts more than I do. When it comes to absolute weight, with twenty-five pounds of additional mass in my favour, I can out lift her in short bursts. But any exercise that requires endurance leaves me looking like an unprepared sprinter part way into a marathon, while she gracefully completes the long series of challenging movements.

On one occasion, while doing squats, I came to appreciate the power of mind over matter. Our trainer, Brian Johnston, who helps us lift our spirits as we lift our weights, was spotting Tania as she attempted her maximum weight. She settled in under the weight, lowered herself into the squat position and then buckled on the way back up, leaving Brian to catch both her and the three hundred pound bar. She was clearly at some limit, physical or otherwise. She took a breather in preparation for a second lift at a lighter weight. To her horror and my amusement, Brian added five more pounds instead. She got under the weight, lowered down and lifted right back up without buckling. Clearly she was not facing a physical barrier as much as a mental one. Brian's positive belief fortified her confidence, and she changed the program of doubt that had been running through her mind.

It is often not the physical and external limitations that we struggle to overcome as much as the internal and mental kind. We can often develop greater power by strengthening our resolve and adjusting our frames of mind than by attempting to make a material shift to the environment or our approach to it. Our belief systems, be they affirmative or negative, may explain more of our forward progress, or lack of it, than our pure technique or tactics. Context may indeed determine content, and what we do may have less impact than what we think. As we believe, so shall our results flow.

I became conscious of one such belief, an apparently wise but extremely dangerous notion that for years I had been operating my business in accordance with: "failure is the best teacher." The belief is logical and tempting: success comes from good judgment, good judgment comes from experience and experience is most often the result of bad judgment. This leads inevitably to the conclusion that I had to fail enough times before I could succeed. And so I did. Following this program led me to enough unfulfilling results and experiences that I decided to change the program to something more workable: "success is the best teacher." And now it is.

In my work with entrepreneurs struggling to overcome stress and make changes for the better, we eventually face the undermining will of a system of limiting beliefs. Over the years, I have culled out and documented an impressive collection of these unworkable positions: "good things take time", "I am a fraud", "I am incompetent", "I am not deserving", "I am not good enough", "I am not qualified", "I am not worthy", "I cannot trust myself or other people", "I have nothing good to offer", "I have to do everything myself", "I have to give up something to get something", "if I accept support I am weak", "it has to be a certain way", "It has to be hard", "it is never good enough", "nothing I do or say makes a difference", "people are fundamentally bad", "people are not capable of doing anything without me", "something better might come along",. "there is not enough to go around", "things never go to plan", "this will never work", "when I reach my dream I die."

There is a countervailing affirmative position for each negative one. *Affirmative beliefs play out as constructive results and experiences and eventually reverse the pattern of self-limiting thoughts and the miserable outcomes they imply.*

Venture Styles 23
Building the Right Type of Business

As a younger entrepreneur, I was convinced that in order to be an entrepreneur I had to build the kind of business I read about in magazines and text books. The business press and business writers traditionally report on only one kind of entrepreneurial venture: the highly original, fast growth type. These are businesses that have developed some breakthrough proprietary technology, hire thousands of keen people, go public and make all the founders millionaires: Ford, GE, 3M, IBM and more recently Microsoft, Cisco, Starbucks and AOL. These are the most famous, most classic examples of great entrepreneurs, creating large successful growth companies. It is easy to judge oneself as incompetent, unintelligent and other wise incapable by the failure to start one of these kinds of enterprise. The reality is, however, that most entrepreneurs do not create such enterprises but nonetheless form the backbone of commercial activity in the economy. Networks of smaller ventures represent the bulk of employment and contribute important innovations to the fabric of society. Most businesses will never attain high levels of fame and fortune but are still very satisfying and fulfilling to their founders and clients.

There are many styles of ventures. Some fit certain entrepreneurs better than others. A venture style reflects the orientation a person has along two dimensions. The first dimension reflects creative orientation, whether they tend to view the creative act as the invention of something better or the better application of existing ideas. Along this dimension someone would choose either to originate an innovation or operate one. The second dimension reflects growth orientation, whether they prefer fast, deep and high-impact growth or slower growth towards greater breadth, balance and lifestyle. Along this dimension, a venture is working towards either greater impact or greater flexibility. Depending on their natural orientations and preferences, each entrepreneur has a primary mode of business operation, as an artist, freelancer, networker or franchisor.

Flexible originators are "artists" whose primary driver is self-expression through commerce. Many designers, inventors, writers and speakers fit into this venture style. Good artists develop an eager audience that appreciates the special content of the business.

Flexible operators are "freelancers" whose primary driver is freedom and variety in work assignments. Most self-employed consultants and contractors are freelancers. Good freelancers develop a consistent flow of clients, time and cash to level out periods of feast or famine.

Impactful operators are "networkers" whose primary driver is rolling out a proven business model quickly through a population of customers. Strong venture managers, network marketers, marketing and sales companies and franchise operators are networkers. Good networkers develop committed support of all business stakeholders.

Impactful originators are "franchisors" whose primary driver is to develop a powerful system that is easily repeatable. Most technology businesses and "classic" startups seek to franchise themselves. Good franchisors develop a functional interface that is easy for all delegates to work.

The ventures I have found most rewarding reflect my artistic nature. It turns out that I am far happier in a creative, lifestyle-oriented business. I have no partners or staff. I work four days a week, and every client represents a new creative adventure. *A venture type that honours an entrepreneur's creative and growth orientations is easier, more fun and less stressful to create and manage successfully.*

The business consultant Fernando Flores believes that our language betrays our true attitudes to the commitments we make. Certain language structures suggest that we genuinely intend to fulfill our promises. Other language suggests we do not own our commitments or the results that arise from our intentions. I take the position that my results are results of my intentions, whether I am conscious of them or not and whether they are positive or not. As I change the language I use, I signal a shift in my subconscious; I feel more powerful, strengthen my commitments and manifest better outcomes.

The first type of powerful language is the first person voice. Many people have slipped into the lazy use of the second person view point, when they are actually referring to themselves: "You work your whole life, because you believe what you do actually matters to someone; and, then, one day you wake up and find you have become redundant." This person's frequent use of "you" when he means "I" suggests to me that he has disowned his thoughts and feelings on the matter, and, worse, he risks having me think he is actually making a judgment about me.

A second focus is on affirmative language. This means eliminating double negatives like "I am disinclined to disagree with you" and pejorative disability language like "I can't seem to get him to stop doing this or that." Another subtle form is the statement, "I have to find a way to make him see my point." Actually, "I do not 'have' to do anything, but I 'want' to." The latter rephrasing puts the thought into language of choice. The most insidious form of negative language is the normative form, which is either prescriptive or proscriptive: "you should do this" or "you should not do that" – to which people likely ask, "is that a fact?" Normative language makes another person the actor.

Grounded language solves the habit of jumping to judgments or assumptions. A sales person might state, "I feel that you just don't get it", implying that a prospect is unwise or ignorant in rejecting a proposal. Grounding means checking out facts and giving people feedback about what we saw or heard: "I heard you say you were not interested in my offer; does that mean 'not ever' or just 'not right now?'" or "I saw what I thought was a puzzled look on your face; have I left some important information out?" Grounded language clears the confusion between sensing, thinking and feeling. Someone might say, "I sense that you are unhappy", when they really mean, "I saw you frowning and thought you were unhappy." Sensing is perceptual: the senses of sight or hearing. Thinking is a cognitive function. People might also say, "I feel you are undermining me", when they really mean, "When I saw you applying for the job I wanted, I thought you were undermining me, and I felt angry." Feeling is an affective function: emotions of happiness, sadness and anger.

The fourth language style is present-tense language. When making a commitment, people often use the future tense and say, "I will complete this action step." The rephrasing, "I am completing this action step," states it as an action that is happening now, not as something that might happen in the future.

The fifth and most subtle form of ownership language is the active voice. A comment like "something should be done about that" is both normative and passive in voice. There is no actor. The implication is that I think someone else ought to do something about what is morally offensive to me. Had I said, "I am doing something about that", I just might do so. When I use the active voice, I place myself front and center in the action so there is a clear path from my thinking to my results.

When we use first-person, affirmative, grounded, present-tense and active voice, we feel powerful, establish powerful intentions and create powerful results.

Living Without Compromise

The comedian Jerry Seinfeld once quipped, referring to a poll that revealed people had a greater fear of public speaking than of death: "that means people would rather be in the coffin than give the eulogy."

On September 5, 2000, I gave the eulogy for one of my best friends: Karl Nagy, a mountain guide, killed suddenly in the prime of his life, doing precisely what he loved and was meant to do. Karl pursued without fear and without compromise his dream of working in the mountains. He was more than just a mountain guide. He brought people back with a sense of being "more alive" – lots of people as it turned out.

What made that day of particular interest to me was both the number of people that turned out to honour the 36-year-old guide and my own reaction to an audience that big. I had always lived somewhat vicariously through Karl, experiencing the life I had flirted with, but not chosen. I had chosen, instead, to work with entrepreneurs. And this meant writing and speaking in public.

Nothing frightened me more than the thought of speaking in front of a large group of people, of being stripped down in public, of baring everything and my soul to an audience who would not care, and worse, who would attack me for being a fraud with nothing important to say. As I spoke to the more than 500 people, guided by Karl's strong spirit and the recollection that I had never seen Karl afraid in the mountains, I found that I too was not afraid. I gained the valuable experience of facing the fear of speaking in public.

I have come to think that no matter what we fear – rejection, failure, success, attack – they can all be reduced to one elemental, animal terror: the fear of death. Death had been an intellectual concept to me. At 36 years of age, and apart from some elderly relatives and a family pet, death had never come calling this close to me before. As climbers, it was a fate we all knew was possible but rarely gave a voice. It was the silent threat. I had tried to deny its existence but only ended up compromising important parts of my life. In trying to avoid feeling the pain of loss and destruction, I had lost touch with the feeling of joy that comes simply from engaging in opportunities to create. In my fear, I had forgotten how to stand up straight on my own stage.

I think spirituality exists in humanity simply because we are all going to die, and we all know it. Our spirit is the motivating force that drives us to create, to find our courage and overcome our fear, and, ultimately, in the face of death, to live. This is what I found in front of a large audience, who did not attack, but who were moved by my words, as they were moved by our friend Karl. In letting my feelings of loss be visible to a crowd of strangers, I rediscovered my deep feeling of joy. Psychologists have a name for this kind of wake-up call: a boundary experience. It happens when we have a close brush with death. We peer over the edge and we can no longer deny its existence. When we come up close to death, we find our spirit and we come out of it. We come out of it alive.

Karl Nagy had a passion for engaging all of the possibilities of life. His gift to me and the gift of his passing has been for me to engage the possibilities of mine. Ironically, I did not find death on that stage. I spoke from the heart and I found life. I found the heart of my venture. *When we find the courage to engage the possibilities life has for us, we move past our fears and create lives rich with meaning and fulfillment that inspire other people to do the same.*

Part II: Integration
Building Common Ground

Creating Connection and Higher Consensus

Darwinian biology, chemistry and physics teach us that there are two opposing forces in the universe – entropy and complexity. Entropy denotes a system's tendency towards greater randomness, decay and disintegration: a drive towards a stable, but possibly boring steady state. These are the forces seeking to reduce beautiful mountain ranges and lush valleys to monotonously flat plains.

Complexity, like human consciousness, denotes a system's tendency towards greater structure, growth and integration: a drive towards a less stable but ultimately more interesting and higher-margin state of innovation. Every innovation at some time in its life becomes stale, worn-out or obsolete and is replaced by something more robust and valuable, that will itself be replaced in the future. These are the cycles of life. Life is more complex and faceted than it was long ago.

Ultimately, if a business endures, it does so because the entrepreneurs design durable and flexible structures to withstand the erosive forces of technology, competitors and customers. A business thrives when it refines its structure and becomes more sophisticated in its adaptations to a threatening environment.

The traditional and narrow view of structure focuses only on the operating system – "how we do it around here" – the organization of people, technology and machines. This view is task and action-centered. Good systems create leverage and power by reliably delivering what is expected by customers. Yet systems are only part of the structure of the enterprise.

The other useful structures of a company are its brand, culture, product and capital structure. In this sense, "structure" is any foundational part of the business that endures.

The brand reflects the identity of the business, what is stands for and what it holds to be most important. The brand is everything that a company presents to a potential client, staffer, supplier or investor. It conveys integrity and trust and attracts people to the venture. A brand is the written, graphical and architectural language of the company, depicting its character and personality. A good brand becomes a vital "virtual person."

The culture is the complex system of both affirmative and limiting beliefs held by the people in the company. Into the social fabric of the company, founders install both their positive beliefs like "there is always a way" and "there is good in everything" and negative beliefs like "it has to be hard" and we are not worthy." They are like an invisible mist that silently inspire or undermine the eventual performance of the organization. When the entire organization becomes conscious of their shared beliefs they can consciously change their minds and take positive positions that work. This ultimately boosts morale and makes the venture more agreeable to work in.

The product is the package of deliverables, everything a client buys or takes possession of and has both tangible and intangible features. The product becomes a structure when human man-hours, technology and an astute understanding of the lives of customers unite. Such a package is satisfying to both the company and the clients.

Finally, the capital structure of a company is the composition of securities and agreements that reimburse all parties for their contributions. Capital reflects not just share and stock structure for investors but the pricing scheme and the balance of the pay and incentives of all people "invested" in the firm, including employees. Here, all stakeholders profit.

Each company endures the disintegrating forces of changing technology, intensifying competition and whimsical customers by building an attractive brand, agreeable culture, deliverable system, satisfying product and profitable capital structure.

The decades after the second world war were a time of great prosperity for North America. The war, which had been an insulator from the poverty and anguish of the Great Depression, resulted in the build up of unprecedented industrial capacity. Entrepreneurs and capitalists made a successful conversion of the military machinery and consumerism was borne. Newly-monied families bought everything that the factories turned out. It was a seller's market, and manufacturers did not need to pay any sort of attention to customer service, value for money, quality or good design.

During the '60s and '70s the modern coercive salesman was born, as was the discipline of consumer psychology. These were modern responses to the simultaneous increase in industrial capacity and productivity and the decline in demand as the distribution pipelines filled. Both sales coercion and consumer psychology sought the same end – to motivate a prospective customer to buy. History, of course, has taught us the futility of trying to manipulate consumers into a "yes" during the time of sale. All that happens is that they return what ever it is they bought for a full refund, and they badmouth the company and destroy the vulnerable base of good will that drives referrals.

Contemporary psychology suggests that we cannot really motivate people to buy, only invoke the motivation they already possess. This means there are prospects who are naturally motivated to buy from us and prospects who are not. Attempting to enroll the latter is just an exercise in misery. Somewhere in the late '70s and '80s, writers such as Theodore Levitt, Phil Kotler and Jay Levinson began to develop the "marketing concept." Chief among their tenets were the notions of segmenting and target marketing. The social sciences provided a scientific basis for this in demography, psychography and ethnography. The idea is to focus creative efforts on a specific group of consumers rather than spreading limited resources attempting to satisfy everyone.

For me, all of these ideas come together in the notion of the core client – the group I was borne to serve. It is only a core client who is naturally interested in what I have to say and offer. Core clients are dream clients or "A" list clients. A look through any client roster reveals some dream clients. They are easy to spot because we are naturally more attracted to them than any others. Core clients are easier to attract, easier to enroll, easier to serve, easier to satisfy, easier to get referrals from and easier to keep for longer periods of time. They are more fun and more lucrative. They are the kind of people we could build a business around and would love to have more of.

A values mesh is what differentiates a core client from all other prospective clients. A high mesh means that a prospect has a naturally high degree of appreciation for my set of values, that we have many values in common. Values are ultimately what motivates any sale. Prospects either share them or they do not. If, for example, I value building common ground and my prospects do not, I will not be able to interest them in becoming my clients simply because they are not interested in what I am. Building common ground is a vital part of my work with entrepreneurs. If I were to trick a person into buying, he or she would eventually become dissatisfied by my attempts to create greater integration. It is not a criticism of either party involved in a values mismesh; it just means that each would be happier in a different relationship. If, however, certain people are really attracted to a set of values, they will likely be very happy as clients. *Ultimately, we cannot fake or manufacture the meshing of values between company and client; we can only sort the clients who are naturally motivated by our value set from the clients who are not.*

Moving Towards the Natural Selection of Customers

Ask any service entrepreneur and they will tell you that some people are easier to serve than others, some are more fun and some are certainly more lucrative. There are people who make better clients than others just as there are people who make better mates than others.

Jay Levinson, was among the first writers to make a connection between marketing and sex, likening the courtship afforded by a marketing conversation as being conceptually not much different than that between two people falling in love. Whether we are speaking about a service provider potentially serving a client or two people investigating the merits of romantic union, the relationship process may be indeed analogous. And the purpose of "marketing" in both cases is precisely the same. Whether one is out looking for new clients or a potential mate, it is, in the end, about attracting the best people.

In mechanical and biological terms, such attraction is genetic. As juicy and romantic as the process of falling in love feels, at some level it is a conversation between two people's DNA. And the conversation is all about the quality and viability of the progeny. This does not explain all attraction between people but it does describe the essential creative act: the procreative act. We naturally screen out candidates with a poor genetic match. Such is the process of natural selection.

Barbara Marx Hubbard made an interesting distinction between two different types of creative energy: procreative and co-creative. The latter is about the attraction of building something with someone. It does not matter in this sense whether the project or progeny is romantic, biological, social or cultural. In service terms this means attracting clients with whom we can build something interesting and good. If I have a service business, my vital function is far more than performing perfunctory tasks for someone as if I were a robot. Service is much more interesting if I see my business as an instrument of co-creation. Between me or any of the people that work for me and each one of our potential or existing clients lies a project, a purpose, something to build together.

Service then, regardless of whether it is the practice of accounting, law, engineering, dentistry or retail selling, is about creating value with someone – not just for someone. This means we can elevate the collaborative process into the spiritual realm by seeing each potential client as a soul mate." If people's souls are the sources of their creativity, then working together to create value becomes a much more sublime experience.

In business we use phrases like "add value" or "the value proposition", but those are often empty phrases of business jargon. I think the purpose of business is to create value with people, whether they are staff or clients. Such value is personal and is the precursor to economic value.

Our best prospective clients, just like our best prospective romantic mates, are those candidates with whom we have the most intimate meshing of core values and the best DNA connection. If core values are those driving motives behind what we are really endeavouring to create, it makes sense to choose people that we share values with. It is from this place of mutual drive that we co-create. My best clients appreciate my values of authenticity, integration, elegance and contribution. These core values reflect the DNA of my company. If my marketing then reflects these values, I attract the right kind of people and repel the people who do not naturally value what I do. People who do not share my values are not bad people, they are just customers who might fit better with my competitors. This is how marketing selects for the best core customers. Our core clients have the same internal drives as we do and so the work is easy, fun and lucrative.

Creating a System of Modular Services and Products

In the middle and late 19th century there were a series of great expositions, notably in London and New York. These expositions captivated their attendees with machines of the coming industrial age. The industrial age, which hit its peak and began to decline in the late twentieth century, had at its core the theme of "efficiency from standardization." The great achievements of the modern age all featured this theme: Colt's first use of interchangeable parts in its gun manufacture, Ford's rationalization of the assembly line and Edison's invention of research and development. Science, rationality, objectivity and uniformity were the pillars upon which the great industrialists built the modern world we now live in.

Prior to the Industrial Revolution, the process of buying, selling, making, using and funding were simple but inefficient. Almost all business was done in a literal, physical market, usually between two people playing all the roles. If a person decided they needed a new pot, they went to the market and sought out a potter whose wares they found attractive. The buyer/user would then tell the seller/maker what they wanted, they would strike a deal and the maker made what the user wanted to use. All articles were custom made in this fashion. This is the origin of the word customer: "the person who wants what they want." Of course the problem with this was the high cost of purely manual, one-off production, meaning that the buyer overpays and the maker under profits.

England and America were the first nations to begin mechanizing and automating production. This required a more massive system of production and marketing and a division of labour. In time, the seller, maker and funder split into more specialized functional areas that ultimately became the modern multifunctional corporation prevalent in the 1970s and 1980s.

The increase in industrial scale required to lower costs led ultimately to the aggregation of user/buyers into groups with uniform characteristics. Mass-marketing pushed the products of the mass-manufacturing onto the masses who were hungry to equip their lives with all the accoutrements of modern life. This worked particularly well in the years immediately following World War II, when demand for merchandise was so high that people would buy anything. But, in the late 1980s, efficiency and standardization became boring for many people. Any mass produced product is by its definition a compromise, satisfying the lowest common denominator. Increasing the size of the mass, increases the compromise. The uniform products and industrial designs that had satisfied their coarser material needs could not satisfy the more subtle and perhaps even more spiritual needs of consumers. Industrial production had made owning products more efficient for the masses, but it had not made owning products more effective at satisfying individual customers.

The current postindustrial age is a return to the intimate and intricate market conversations possible in the pre-industrial age. The Internet, flexible manufacturing and mass-customization allow people to get what they want without sacrificing efficiency. Dell Computer is a notable example of a company that efficiently gives customers precisely what they want by assembling custom products from standard modules.

Most service providers sell their time inefficiently on a one-off basis, in the pre-industrial way. *A modular approach allows a service provider to make some reasonable assumptions about what most people need, build some standard discrete modules and then assemble them in unique ways to meet the differing needs of each customer.* A modular approach balances customer whims against their need for economy. This lowers costs by making it easier to duplicate standard service items and increases prices because customers are getting what they want. Margins increase from both directions.

Inviting Stakeholders into the Creative Process

Chief among the tenets of the environmental design school I attended was the idea that any object whether it is a small consumer product or a city ought to respect its environment. The environment is not just the physical and natural environment. To an enterprise, there are a number of important social, cultural, technical and economic environments to consider. The environment is the context in which a venture works in, defined by people who will buy, sell, serve, use and fund the enterprise. Environmental design means designing a business to work for the buying environment, the selling environment, the serving environment, the using environment and the funding environment. These environments are by definition the external influences on a venture.

The word "environment" means "the space around the mind." The creative process most of us go through to create and design our ventures is often a very private, very personal process that happens primarily in our own minds. This view of creativity is an inside-out process, where we are working to express some idea or contribution. Much invention happens this way, but the objects of such a process often do not work for the people that eventually have to buy, sell, serve, use or fund them. Stakeholders often have little say in how a final product emerges from development and the "creator" often acts surprised when they reject the business model.

The inside-out creative process has the advantage of having the expert in a particular field – the entrepreneur – anticipate trends, technologies and problems and configure solutions. Often clients do not know they want or need something until the very moment they see it. The new product or service wakes up some dormant, nearly conscious itch in need of scratching. The problem with a strict inside-out model is a combination of arrogance and fantasy. It is easy to believe that a customer needs and would want to pay handsomely for some new creation when that is just not the case. Many business failures result from over-exuberant entrepreneurs over-estimating the willingness of stakeholders to buy into a limited view of the world.

A participatory design process balances the push model of inside-out creativity with the pull model of outside-in creativity. The powerful internal creative force meets the powerful external creative force. The products of such development marry the expert judgments of entrepreneurs with strong feedback from stakeholders.

There are several methods of obtaining feedback from stakeholders. The point is not so much to directly ask people what they want; this usually works poorly precisely because creation is a process focused on future needs, which may or may not be clear to people at the time. Early in the process, anthropological-like methods allow us to observe what is going on in the lives of people we may ultimately serve. This provides a basic context in which to design new business models and concepts: scenarios or stories about of how the business could work differently with new marketing, selling, organization, service or finance designs. Focus groups, depth interviews and on-line test websites are ways to put the scenarios in front of people for their evaluation and creative input. Such input is useful in the process of designing prototypes and the live retail beta test. This pilot test places a new business model in front of real prospects in a controlled fashion to measure and validate the new venture prior to final launch, while many details are still malleable and adjustable.

Stakeholder feedback and input during the design process move us out of fantasy and arrogance and into making our ventures work better for buyers, sellers, servers, users and funders.

A Thing of Beauty
Appreciating the Good Support of the People Close to Us

My wife grew up in an entrepreneurial family and luckily
seemed to know precisely what she was getting into when she
married me. Her father is a brilliant scientist and her mother
has a strong back bone that has held their family together
through the periods of rise and fall that beset all entrepreneurial ventures. My wife, has sacrificed many things
important to her and endured some stressful moments to support
the business. Like most entrepreneurial families, we have had
to juggle bills, periodically do without certain material
comforts, cancel holidays and live with the ambiguity of not
always knowing whether the bank card transaction was going
to return "approved" or if the store clerk was going to say, "I
am sorry your credit card has been declined."

Throughout the many challenges of building a successful
business, a spouse is far more than the person behind the
entrepreneur. Whether or not they literally help in the
running of the business, spouses are active partners in the
business. Not only do they technically own half of what the
entrepreneur does, a supportive spouse provides an environment
in which an entrepreneur is much freer to go out and create
innovations. During the toughest years of our business, Tania
has been the grounding force in our lives. Not only has she kept
our physical home together, she has worked hard to create a
spiritual and emotional home for us, a safe place to which I
return when I feel defeated and knocked down by the business
world or the people in it. She has created stability for us on
every level, all while managing the stresses and challenges of
her own successful career. Without the gift of her support and
the stability it creates, I would feel less secure, less confident
and less willing to go out into a risky and harsh world.

Our business is working well now because we have
worked together to overcome the challenges of starting and

growing it. Precisely because she is so supportive and selfless, I know that she would be reluctant to take any credit for our successes, but the profits we now enjoy in our lifestyle, the quality of our experience of life and the kind of impact our business is having on customers are as much a result of her sacrifice, good judgment and support as they are of my direct work in the business. I have come much farther in life because she has had the courage and patience to believe in me and tolerate the stress that kind of commitment has generated.

As entrepreneurs if we succeed or fail, we do not do so alone. A venture would be nearly impossible to mount and maintain, if not for the flexibility of the people in our support chain. I have many friends that have given me small loans, physical labour, a well-timed kind word or an equally well-timed kick in the pants. My kids somehow know on stressful days not to act up and have learned to time financial requests around positive cashflow. My parents are always available and want the best for me. I have a large team of coaches and advisors that make themselves available and safe for my ranting and raving about a world that sometimes appears not to want what I have to offer – and they cheer me on as it does. My customers have been willing participants in my many experiments, some of which have worked in their favour and others which have not.

Many entrepreneurs start companies for the power and freedom of self-directed life. But true power is not a solo venture. Such independence is an illusion as fruitless as the enterprise of trying to cut one's own hair. *True power comes not from lone entrepreneurs wielding their creative authority on the naked world but from the grace and courage of a large group of supporters making a safe and stable platform on which to launch their dreams.*

Building Confidence and Preempting Objections in the Sales Process

I think many people would find it strikingly odd and perhaps even offensive to see the words "spirituality" and "selling" in the same sentence. Spirituality for many is a sacred, vulnerable and intensely private matter: "It is none of your business", and it is not to be confused with "business" either. Selling is all business and invokes unfortunate images of manipulation and heartless profit.

The sales job differs according to the item or service. Commodities, which people tend to buy solely on price, do not require the assistance of a well-trained facilitator for their purchase. They require order takers. Higher value purchases, which are more emotional and passionate, require a process for prospective clients to become comfortable with the seller, the service and the supplier.

Jay Levinson unearthed a study looking at why people chose one furniture manufacturer over another. Out of nine factors used to differentiate vendors during these high-end purchases, buyers placed price last and confidence first. It seems buyers expect good quality, beautiful design and great service from every vendor. Reputation, warranties, guarantees and such enhance but do not create confidence. The word confidence comes from Latin meaning "with faith", connoting spirituality. Spirituality has a pragmatic sense to it. By spiritual, I am not speaking necessarily about religion or morality. I mean that a business "has faith" and is spiritual to the extent that it honors its core beliefs.

During the selling process, a company creates and a prospect experiences either confidence or doubt. High-value purchases pose inherently higher risks to the prospect. First, they are more exposed financially to disappointment because the items and services in question have premium prices. Second, as these purchases tend to be more passionate in nature, the buyer is emotionally more vulnerable. An appropriate prospect has a natural meshing of values with the seller, a need or stress arising from the absence of one or more of those values and access to resources to solve the problem. Those conditions make agreement possible and even probable. The rest is a leap of faith.

The enemy of such a leap is doubt. Doubt is an absence of faith and therefore of spirit. A customer can only be as confident in the business as the business is in itself. Doubt undermines confidence and leads to fear, and fear is the enemy of attracting and enrolling customers. I can manufacture objections in the sales process simply by having certain doubts about myself, my business, the service or the future relationship. For example, when I am unsure of myself and thinking that I am not worthy, I induce a painful series of price objections that seem to imply, or rather unquestionably prove, that I am indeed unworthy of the prices I am asking for. When I release this position and instead reconnect with what is special and unique about me, my confidence rises and I stand by my price. Limiting beliefs and self-defeating thoughts communicate doubt to prospective clients, who are then almost required to object to the proposal on the grounds they imply.

Beliefs such as "everyone is special and unique in someway" or "people are basically good" are spiritually-grounded positions. They are not anything I can prove, and neither are they truths in the absolute sense of what that normally means. I can certainly disprove my affirmations if I choose to – there are many examples of mediocre and evil deeds in the world around me – but that kind of thinking only undermines my confidence in myself, my offer and my price. Instead, my affirmative beliefs gain their power simply by my holding of them. In any given moment, I can, as Einstein pointed out, come from fear or faith. Fear and doubt repel. Faith attracts. The job of a sales person in this context is to build confidence. *We close more sales from a place of faith than from a place of doubt and fear.*

The philosopher Pierre Teilhard de Chardin proposed the existence of a collective consciousness – the idea of one shared mind that he called the "noosphere." Many psychologists, including Freud and Jung, have made extensive study of the various levels of the consciousness, including what lies under or below the wide-awake level of full consciousness. Their notions come together in the idea of a shared subconscious. While my consciousness appears to be a function of my five sensory perceptions and I can identify its contents as me personally, my subconscious may be something that I share with others in my proximity and I can only perceive it through a psychic sixth sense.

Many people have had the experience of this otherworldly perception. It shows up most obviously through intuition but also through other prescient faculties such as anticipation, premonition and clairvoyance. I have found it easy to discount my own experiences with this other form of consciousness and to dismiss the accounts I have heard about as quaint metaphysics or worse, as laughable mysticism.

There is much written on the subject and essence of leadership, from the historical to the mechanical. A common thought is that leaders bring about meaningful change in the world. This means that, as entrepreneurs, we are responsible for identifying opportunities and then leading our partners, staff, investors and clients through the innovation process to a place of greater value. Historically, "leader" was synonymous with "prophet". Despite its strong religious connotations, prophets were people who gained the wisdom of a powerful view of the world and led whatever group they were involved in towards its fruition. The word prophecy also denotes a future-tense, implying that prophets were people with gifted foresight. A great entrepreneur, then, is someone who has this gift of foresight and marshals resources in the service of its fulfillment. Entrepreneurs are contemporary prophets, whose enterprise is not one of philanthropy or social activism but one of profits.

A strongly-held view of a potential, more valuable future is a prophecy. A limiting belief such as "this will not work" or "no one is going to buy this" is also a prophecy. It is a view of the future but features a negative result. If I take those unworkable positions, my experience is they will manifest themselves precisely as the negative results they imply: the undertaking will not work or no one will buy it. This is a self-fulfilling prophecy – an intention – that works equally well in the affirmative.

I take the position that my results are the results of my intentions, whether conscious or not, and whether positive or not. For example: I enroll every customer I intend to. If someone says "yes" it is because we share a conscious, positive intention to create value together; if someone says "no", it is because one of us has made a strong negative, unconscious intention to sabotage the relationship. A strong "yes" trumps a weak "no" and vice versa. This is not necessarily true, in the absolute sense, but I have noticed that my closing rates have gone up and my sales cycle time has gone down since I made the conscious intention to make more money in less time.

I think that I "store" my intentions in the collective subconsciousness. I call this is my ground. Common ground is the sum of both positive, conscious intentions and negative, unconscious intentions shared by me and people in my presence. When my ground is weak, I hold a substantial number of limiting beliefs and unworkable positions that undermine my larger vision and lead to miserable results. *When our ground is strong, we have taken a predominance of workable positions that support us to create the positive results we intend, with the support of the people in our presence.* That is the essence of leadership.

Integrating the Form and Function of Service

Curators at the Philadelphia Museum of Art once asked two great designers their opinions of what constituted good design. The German Max Bill said, "good design depends on the harmony established between the form of an object and its use." The Modernist German tradition places the ideal of utility above all else. The clean, unencumbered lines of a Porsche 911 or a Braun kitchen appliance reflect the German love of rational, unadorned styling tending towards uniformity and standardization. The modern notion of goodness in design, ethics or politics is that of an objective truth, more to be discovered than created.

The idea that there is only one standard to judge the moral worth of something offends many people subscribing to a more liberal and pluralistic view of the world. When the Italian Ettore Sottsass voiced his opinion on the same question, he said, "that supposes that somewhere, somehow, there is a place where good design is deposited." To Sottsass, good design would be best defined by the people experiencing it. As a Postmodernist, Sottsass would say that the moral quality of any creative product depends on the anthropological frame one puts around it. While there may indeed be broad consensus on the moral or ethical value of an action or artifice, good design is subjective: beauty is in the eye of the beholder. A good service design reflects the people it serves.

Such discussions reflect different notions about the relationship between the form of a product or service and its function. Modernists would say, "form follows function", as a statement that any design product must reflect rational standards of utility. Postmodernists toss out that notion, suggesting that the functions of any product or service ought to reflect its cultural frame. There are no objective measures of value other than those defined by the people in whose life the article fits.

The function of a service is to create value. Personal values such as respect, truth, commitment or excellence are not just convenient concepts or ideals, they can drive the design and operation of a business and all of its structures. The function of a service business reflects the domains in which it operates. The user domain of the business reflects the need for the service to reduce stress and make some aspect of life easier. Every stress represents the absence of some value. Services work when they convert a user's stressful experience into a satisfying one. Where there is the experience of overwhelm there is the opportunity to create the experience of power; where there is the experience of indifference there is the opportunity to create passion. Clarity solves confusion; confidence solves uncertainty; acknowledgment solves invalidation. There is no shortage of stress, and there is no absence of the opportunity to create greater satisfaction. Function reflects the experiential layer of a professional service, whether accounting or architecture, quite distinct from the technical practice of it.

The form of a service is quite different from the form of a physical item. Form in a physical product is easier to consider because there is a material and a physical structure. We base our experience of the built world largely on tangible perceptions of what we can see or touch or hear. An automobile or building is more direct and tangible than the services that create them. These are more difficult to substantiate but no less different to experience.

The general form of a service business is made up of its five structural elements: brand, culture, system, product and capital structure. Whether the service is a high-end retail, accounting, law, financial planning or architectural design practice, these components form the whole structure of the enterprise. *The form of well-designed service reflects its function to deliver on its underlying value proposition.*

My favourite piece of outdoor clothing is made by a company called Patagonia. I use my Guide pants for all of my outdoor pursuits: all varieties of climbing, cycling, and skiing. They are the most versatile product I own. This product does not compromise any of its functions for the sake of others (like it would if someone had stuck a clock in them!) Patagonia started with the vision of Yvon Chouinard, now retired, an industrial designer, environmentalist, entrepreneur, climber and writer. One of his core values is that of "form follows function design." A well-designed garment is clean, durable and has more than one use, allowing people to have fewer garments that each last longer. Patagonia garments are both aesthetically elegant and environmentally sensitive.

The American sculptor Horatio Greenough used the term "form follows function" to denote a functionalist doctrine that the most valuable part of any design is that which makes it useful. In the outdoor clothing world, to say something is functional suggests at once that it works well for its intended purpose and that it is unadorned and without unnecessary fashion styling. My idea of functionality is broader than what something is useful for. Products are complex clusters of values delivering a rich experience. To say that an object is multi-functional and versatile is to say that it has many valences, functions or energy levels apart from its pure utility.

The first function of any product, whether tangible or intangible, is technical. On a hierarchy of value creation and needs satisfaction, basic utility is the foundation and lowest energy level. This first valence describes the product's usefulness as a tool: knives cut, clothing insulates, chairs facilitate sitting, accountants audit and lawyers sue. Good tools are fulfilling and powerful.

The second function is aesthetic and denotes the product as a work of art. A tool does something, but a work of art evokes an emotional experience. This valence describes the product's capacity for beauty. A knife, clothing, chair, audit and lawsuit can be both useful and a work of art. Utility and beauty are not mutually exclusive. Good art is distinctive and passionate.

The third function is cultural. The symbolic qualities of a product reference an important set of values and allow users to express themselves: "This product says something about me, who I am and what is important to me." The referential component of a product may connote its prestige, luxury or certain rituals (like a Saturday morning latte). Good symbols are authentic and clear.

The final function is social. In this valence, the product acts as an invitation to a social group or community of like-minded people. Clothing for snowboarders and skiers is useful to the extent that inhabitants stay dry and warm. The garments may also be beautiful in the way they are constructed or configured or patterned. What the garments express about the individual user may be quite different, but how the product communicates social status and group membership is a final mark of value. Snowboard clothing that invokes a hip hop design language may speak to the young people who make up the largest contingent of snowboarders. Ski clothing, conversely, may be more sophisticated in its styling to reflect the baby boomers who drive the ski business and the sport utility vehicles in the parking lot. Meaningful portals are integrated and connected.

A good product design performs all of its functions well without compromise. *A product that is at once a useful tool, offering great utility; an evocative work of art, offering great beauty; an informative symbol, offering great self-expression; and an inviting portal, offering great access is more valuable than a basic technical commodity.*

In the past ten years, leaders of the corporate world have often cited the attraction and retention of employees as a primary business concern. The terms talent, human capital, human resources all reflect the corporations' hunt for good people and a deeper respect for the employees who create value inside the enterprise. Attracting and retaining employees has become the new marketing challenge.

In the post war economy, arrogant industrialists pushed jobs on employees as they pushed products on consumers. People then were so hungry for growth and prosperity that they readily consumed the products of industry and were willing to do just about anything to earn the money to buy them. Companies built the products and the jobs that surrounded them and then figured out how to sell them to non-discerning consumers and employees alike, all the while profiting from the relationship between the people that made these commodities and the people that bought them.

By the 1980s, consumer demand softened. A spiritual enlightenment took hold, and people discovered that meaningless consumption was not the path to happiness. Global brands that grew up to dominate consumer marketing had to take on a more emotional and spiritual tone to maintain their connections with consumers. Good brands became symbols of real value. As an attempt to continue the profit growth, marketing matured into an industry dedicated to learning what people really wanted and figuring out how to deliver it to them. Instead of building something and then pushing it on people, companies discovered the power of learning what people wanted first. What they built for people would then pull them in. Mass customization of products accompanied deft one-to-one style marketing, and individual consumers got largely what they imagined they wanted.

The shift from push to pull marketing was a transfer of power from the manufacturer, who historically decided the offering, to the consumer, who had by now discovered that they could decide what they wanted to buy. The Internet and a decade of communications innovation have amplified this power, and, surprisingly, the good global brands have kept pace – or they have perished. Now, there are so many choices, and the future is changing so rapidly, that consumers often do not know what they want or even need. So finally, the consumer and corporation have achieved a balanced model of push-pull: the corporation interprets future technology and innovates within the context of a powerful consumer base; consumer and corporation, in effect, design the product together.

A company's relationships with its employees may well be following a similar path. The demand for many companies' jobs has also softened. The same spiritual enlightenment has led people to discover that meaningless work is not a path to happiness either. It is no longer viable to push a job on someone and hold dominion over them. A paycheck is no longer a bill-of-sale. Like their powerful consumer analogs, employees are coming to appreciate the massive scope of their choices in employment. A good consumer brand binds consumers in a trust relationship that is driven by a powerful set of core values. A good employer brand will come to do the same.

Employees are demanding more meaningful jobs, just as consumers have learned to demand more meaningful products; each party will seek out "suppliers" who can design the "products" they want to buy. A smart company mass-customizes its products to fit the idiosyncrasies and whims of its consumers. *Good corporations treat each job like a product designed to meet the special needs of its consumer – a powerful employee who has the ultimate power to change vendors if the quality, service and price do not fit his or her needs.*

People are social creatures. Our gregarious natures drive us to congregate in all sorts of groups and networks. While some people are introverted and others are extroverted, we all identify with some community that in some way reflects our thinking, values and systems of shared experience. Such an organization could be a literal club or association or a subculture within society, such as "people with university degrees" or "bird watchers" or "travelers"; even members of the subgroup "people who like to do things by themselves" share that desire and thinking with other like minds. Any community is a collection of like minds gathered together for some common purpose, and communities of customers who share a sense of spirit and values are no exception.

There was a lot of talk about building on-line communities during the explosive years of the Internet. I do not know how successful these attempt were, but I suspect that many were unsuccessful because they merely threw money into expensive media without harnessing the collective spirit of a group of people isolated from each other. Communities require a strong and compelling purpose to knit them together and a strong and compelling evangelist to enroll them in it.

Guy Kawasaki, as a pioneer of Apple Computer, was perhaps the first formal business evangelist. His job was to travel around and get programmers and media people excited about the Macintosh platform and what the company stood for, rallying them around the larger purpose of providing a viable alternative to the Wintel stranglehold. Without the buy-in of programmers and the media, there would be no Mac-native applications and no one would be able buy Apple hardware.

While the word "evangelist" has religious con-notations, it has now come to mean "inspiring buy-in" to a company platform of values and purpose. Evangelists inspire customers to inspire other customers, together creating a shadow sales force and a large, interconnected network of customers. Since this sales force works only for the experience of connection and not money, it can be an efficient way to enroll new customers. Its power derives from the geometry of network math. In the early stages, there are fewer connections between people: the network is small and slow growing. Then it hits critical mass, the connections between people multiply and the population explodes.

Inspiring buy-in means "encouraging people to enroll into the spirit of the venture." The spirit of the venture lies in its world view, its reason for being and its calling. From this perspective, business is not a series of lifeless commercial transactions. It is a deeper connection between kindred spirits. A world view describes the bigger picture and the lifetime contribution of a company to its people and the world around it. The products themselves and their underlying technology are only material, momentary and not enough to keep people permanently bonded to the company.

What keeps clients loyal for life is a connection to what the company stands for – its underlying spiritual orientation. My interpretation of the world view of Apple is to create a world of individual free expression, where creativity and innovation make life easier and more beautiful. I bought into that spirit, and I have stayed loyal to Apple, even during the years when they were struggling and producing junky PC-clones. I have put great effort into enrolling people into the platform. Mac users are not merely customers, they are a global community of creative people dedicated to making the world different. *When people buy into the larger world view and deeper spirit of the enterprise, they form an interconnected community of loyal supporters actively working to expand the community by enrolling more people.*

Taking the Risk Out of Buying

Traditional views of buyer behaviour depict a rational consumer following a rational process. A typical consumer would analyze their needs, set about to research which alternative products and services might solve the problem, evaluate each against a set of weighted criteria and then purchase the alternative that faired best on the score sheet. I do not remember the last thing I bought like that. The rational consumer model completely ignores the force of emotions during the process of purchasing. A more accurate picture is the irrational consumer who is drawn to purchase something, maybe assesses alternative solutions, makes an emotional choice and then uses the powers of intellect and logic, after the fact, to justify the purchase and dissipate the strain of cognitive dissonance or buyer's remorse. People may fall closer to the rational side during the purchase of an ordinary commodity, but when the area is personal and passionate, the emotions take over.

Pet shops have known and exploited this fact for years. The purchase of a little kitten or puppy is no more rational than two people falling in love. So pet shops offer to let the family try out the new potential family member and bring them back if they change their minds. I can imagine how few animals get returned back to the store once they have left in the loving arms of a small child.

The selection of a special pet to join a family is likely not a commodity purchase. In a commodity purchase, there are few emotions and buyers buy based on the lowest price they can find. For higher-value passion purchases, the buyers purchase not on price but confidence – the trust the buyer develops in the product and the company they are buying from. Brian Tracy and Jay Abraham are both proponents of taking the risk out of the buying process – of being the "low risk producer" and "reversing the risk", rather than lowering prices to simulate that trust.

The approach to confidence building, rather than price lowering, applies differently to tangible products and intangible services. A prospect experiences physical products literally during the selling process: through a test drive, try-on, photograph or even their ability to "drink in" the aesthetics of the product because they can see, feel, hear, taste or smell it. These emotional-aesthetic experiences and supporting money back guarantees and warranty programs afford security and confidence. For many service providers, especially those of us offering expensive, high-end services, the buyer's perceived purchasing risk can be very high. Services are more ethereal and experiential than tangible products, and the client will not truly "feel" the benefits of a service until after they agree to buy it. If we leave buyers only to their rational understanding of our offers, they might not have enough emotional connection to risk a higher-price purchase.

Samples of high-price, high-passion services lower the perceived risk of purchase by creating strong emotional connections between the buyer and service provider. A sample gives future users a clear and emotionally evocative glimpse of the real salient benefits of ownership, prior to commitment. It is valuable in its own right, independent of the follow-on service. Guarantees and warranties and the positive energy of the sellers all work to support the connection made during the precommitment trial. After the gift of the sample, the value is no longer intellectual or theoretical. It is felt and very real. While I intend to close every viable sale and make the details work for each buyer, the sample is a pure contribution. I cannot fake the concern I feel for a client during a sample. Because my first offer and concern is to give something away without the expectation of results, prospects experience my attractive positive energy. It simply communicates: "My first priority here is to be of service to you." The deal takes care of itself.

Finding the Shortest Path to the Right People

In *The Tipping Point,* author Malcolm Gladwell describes the derivation of the phrase "six degrees of separation" in the experiments of psychologist Stanley Milgram, undertaken to understand the "small world" phenomenon. Milgram sent 160 packets to anonymous residents of Omaha, Nebraska. The packet contained the instructions to forward the packet on to a friend or acquaintance they thought could mail it closer to a stockbroker who worked in Boston, also drawn at random. Even if the friend or acquaintance did not know the stockbroker, they themselves might be able to mail it one step closer, until finally someone in the chain did, in fact, know the target person. By analyzing the postmarks of the mail received by the stockbroker, Milgram learned that no piece of mail needed more than six hops. Six degrees of separation means that we are no more than six introductions away from the ideal clients we seek.

One of my favourite seminar activities is to model this affect by placing six people in a row. I whisper a phrase into the ear of the first one; that person then whispers the same phrase to the next person, as best as he or she can hear and remember it, and so on. This is a model for how the chain of introductions work in a referral chain. The phrase I start with is "eschew obfuscation" – technically complicated jargon that always comes out garbled. The second phrase, which has the same meaning as the first is "be clear." Clear phrases move without friction between people in the chain.

In real life markets, if clarity is what steers information from person to person, then passion is the force that drives it. And indifference kills the flow. Indifference surfaces in the chain as inattention, well-meaning ignorance, philosophical disagreement and, in the extreme case, malicious discontent. Indifference is literally a lack of difference. We create indifference anytime we present ourselves with our passionless technical jargon. Most of us have experienced the classic cocktail party or networking ritual of meeting new people: "Hi, I am so and so, what do you do?" With that prompt comes the standard reply: "I am so and so, and I am an accountant (lawyer, doctor, dentist, designer, financial planner, and so on)."

People are able to make a large number of judgments about us when they first meet us. If I choose to start out by saying, "This is the activity I do that is essentially no different than thousands of other businesses", I get an indifferent response. I have chosen to communicate at a purely technical level and that is just not the most interesting aspect about me. Technically, I coach entrepreneurs. So what. A purely technical introduction provides a necessary but basic and insufficient message. The subject either ignores the intro- duction, misunderstands it or, in the worst case, experiences it as offensive. People just do not care enough to pass that lifeless piece of information around: "Did you hear the news? That guy over there is an accountant!"

Something far more meaningful and far more interesting is passion. Passion creates cash-flow, joy, repeat business, referrals and jobs. Passion is more than technology and products. My passion is assisting professional entrepreneurs in creating higher purpose and higher profit. This idea is core to my being. When I add this phrase to my introduction and express the passion behind it, people connect with me and my business and spread the word through a chain to the right people.

Each of us is interesting. People are attracted to our passion. We have the opportunity to say something meaningful every time we tell our story to prospective new clients. *When we speak from the heart, about what is most important to us, the right people listen, the right people show up and the right people buy.*

Making Space for a Sale   40
Helping Prospects Volunteer to be Clients

My wife is an occupational therapist who works with geriatric patients to assist them in returning to a life of grace after they suffer some sort of stroke, hip fracture or other disempowering incident. Like many therapists, she takes the position that the best way to help someone recover or make any sort of change in their lives is to empower them to do so. This often means not doing something for someone, even out of an urge to be helpful, when they are capable of doing it themselves. Such action would create a dependency and lower the person's sense of power. However, it does not mean completely abandoning a person to complete independence prior to the return of their power.

"Respectful intervention" is a moderate approach creating an interdependence between a vulnerable client and a well-trained professional. This method of empowerment acknowledges the boundaries that exist in a professional relationship. A professional person must intervene in peoples' lives to effect any sort of change, but that intervention needs to be done in a way that honours the client in need of the service. It does not work to disengage, and it does not work to intrude.

Nowhere in business is this middle ground so important than in the process of selling. One must serve to sell and all service requires this respectful intervention – the process of empowering people to make choices. If my prospects are not "raising their hands" to be my clients, then I am either "pushing" them away or "not pulling" them closer. I am either disengaging or intruding.

People in service businesses often dislike selling because they judge sales as being somehow pushy or disrespectful. In an honorable attempt to be respectful of prospects, combined with a fear of rejection and a preference for just doing the work, these people never pose nor even imply the closing question "will you buy?" Their thought here is that people will buy on their own, if they see the value. This kind of passive selling or order-taking does not work for sophisticated services.

People hate to be sold and love to buy, but it does take work to think through a purchase. Sometimes people want expert assistance. Selling is just the first phase of service. Rapport building, needs assessment, opportunity identification and creative concept design all occur prior to the moment of formal contracting. When service entrepreneurs separate "selling" and "service", they are less prepared to intervene in the sales process and do not seem open for business. Prospects interpret this as a lack of interest in serving them. The seller, who is pretending not to be a seller, has made no space for the closing question "will you buy?" and therefore has made no space for the answer "yes."

The other extreme is trying to push people into buying. Prospects often experience the enthusiasm behind this approach as aggressive, officious and disrespectful. Not only is the question "will you buy?" explicit, the seller's belief is so strong in their expertise that they expect a "yes!" While that may seem to be just positive thinking, it comes through as dogmatic and arrogant. Because the seller expects to hear a "yes" they really have made no space for the answer "no." Thus the prospect at some unconscious level believes they really have no choice. So they do not choose and stay in a permanent "maybe" position. If they say, "yes", they often withdraw when the pressure is off.

Good sales people empower their prospects to make choices that work for them by being both respectful and enthusiastic. Respect means deferring to the prospects and cultivating the belief that they know best for themselves. This makes space for an honest "yes" or "no" answer to an offer. Enthusiasm is about actually making the offer and cultivating the belief that we know best about our services and what might work to satisfy the client's needs. This makes space for the closing question. Selling is a respectful intervention.

During the startup phase of a new venture, the founding entrepreneurs tend to do everything themselves. It is a labour of love, and they happily work long hours to ensure each detail is handled well. These entrepreneurs design and build the product, they find the clients and they personally make sure every client is happy. When the founders make promises to clients, they personally look them in the eye and shake their hands. The customer buys in and begins what is hopefully a fruitful relationship with the entrepreneur.

If entrepreneurs are successful, they develop a reputation for innovation, and in Tom Peter's vernacular, every client goes, "Wow!" Of course the business grows on the foundation of its early success. The entrepreneurs reach the limit of their time capacity and the need for more leverage, more productivity and systems and staff to do more of the work. Likewise, at the end of their careers, when it is time to retire, the entrepreneurs face the same challenge – transferring control, power, equity and goodwill to their successors.

The transfer is difficult when all of the key business relationships and know-how are stuck with the founder. Succession works only when the company has a brand that works: the goodwill and reputation for Wow! that exists with the client base belong to the company and not the entrepreneur directly. The entrepreneur is free to just work there.

The equity that exists in a brand is goodwill. Goodwill is the feeling of value and confidence and affection that exists among customers towards the company. If customers identify their goodwill with the entrepreneurs and not the company, then the entrepreneurs will be unable to delegate their operations to successors whether at time of growth or exit. They take the relationships with them wherever they go because existing customers are often uncomfortable trusting someone new.   Sustainable identity means that the reputation and goodwill created by the entrepreneur is available to everyone that works for the company. The 3M company is over a century old. Most people cannot name the founders or even a single CEO of 3M, but they identify 3M as innovation. That is the basis of its brand, and it has endured for decades. In such a brand-strong company, the business relationship and reputation exists between the company and the client and not the founder and the client.   The goodwill is sustainable whether the founder still works there or not.

The core values of the founding entrepreneurs define the bedrock of a company's brand and identity. Core values are what the entrepreneurs stand for, what they hold to be most important. When they install these values into the structures of the enterprise, the enterprise takes on a life of its own. In the beginning, clients derive this value from the direct personal service of the entrepreneurs. Eventually, it needs to finds its way into every detail of the company presentation (the aesthetics and stature of websites, brochures, interior designs), culture (shared beliefs), systems (tactical procedures and mechanisms for performing the technical work of the business), products (the offering) and capital (the financial structure including pricing and employee incentives).

Ironically, businesses work better when the founders make themselves redundant and install all of the good will, key business relationships and intellectual property into the business structure. When this happens, even while the founders are still working, a business gains capital value, because someone else could buy or run it successfully and independently. The entrepreneurs have ultimately become interchangeable with their staff. The business can live on past the startup, exit and even death of its founders. That is sustainable identity and true freedom.

Higher Purpose, Higher Profit

Apart from its use as a legal term of art, "partnership" has come to describe any project where people collaborate. By melding their passions into an expression of mutual creativity, partners create something greater than they could do on their own. Collaboration has it roots it Latin, meaning "to work together."

Whether it is with a legally-equal business partner, an ally, staff member or customer, the reality of working with other people is inevitable. These human relationships are the pinnacle of both frustration and joy. At their best, good working partnerships create both synergy, a whole that is greater than the some of its parts, and autonomy, where each player has the freedom to make their contribution and express their value without compromise. At their worst, partnerships become hateful, life-sucking conflict generators that compromise the participants and fail to create any consensus. I have had my share of both.

Partnerships work when they create consensus. Such consensus is an elegant agreement of both values and vision: what is mutually important and defines of the function and form of the relationship. Partnerships breakdown when they create more conflict than consensus. Would-be collaborators destroy consensus, synergy and autonomy when they polarize in their visions about form and structure without first considering values, what is important and why they are even trying to work together.

In a business, the basic partnership is the one between customers and entrepreneur. The customers have stress and money and the desire for joy. The entrepreneur has technology and foresight and the desire for growth. In this situation, one of two scenarios often happens. Either the entrepreneur creates a product that the customers do not want or the customers do not know what they really want and instead request something that is not feasible. Only in their creative collaboration will each party get what they desire.

In design school, we were trained to create manufactured products that people wanted to use and buy. To do that, we needed to release our intellectual positions about what a product really was and look deeper. If we wanted to create a cool chair, we would first ask ourselves, "What is a chair?" or "Which kind of chair would that user really want?" Formally, a chair is a flat platform, back and four legs. Holding on to this rather limited vision, we would create nothing innovative. What is more interesting is the relationship a person has with the object. So, conversely, if we asked, "Why do they want a chair?" or "How does this chair need to work?", we would identify the functions of "reclining in comfort", "expressing personal taste" or "reflecting the appropriate social status." If entrepreneur and customer can first come to a consensus on this level – the true value of the creation – then there is an opportunity to create a new vision and a new form. These functional requirements drive the definition of the "problem space" and are a precondition for people getting into a creative "solution space".

The same method holds true for any partnership of people trying to create something new and innovative. Not every partnership seems destined to work, but prospective partners with the intention and spirit of goodwill can create synergy and autonomy. *If we ask the "why" and "how" questions of function before the "what" and "which" questions of form, we have the best chance of reconciling our values and creating a shared vision that honors everyone without compromise.* Form follows function.

Integrating the Architecture of the New Economy

Several decades ago, an unlikely group of people inadvertently predicted the emergence of the so-called New Economy and Information Age. Those people were architectural critics.

Architecture draws the most critical debate of any other part of the built world simply because of the durability and conspicuity of its product. A big, ugly, unusable building is a problem for more than just its inhabitants. People from within a large radius also suffer its aesthetic indignation. Thus a lot of thought has been put into the whole architectural enterprise with the intent to suffuse it with foresight, responsibility and respect. And the people who create and critique architecture often take the long view, anticipating major social, cultural and technological trends in the process.

In the sixties, architecture, government and business were thoroughly modern, drawing their organizing inspirations from the machine, science and rationality. Every institution featured centralized planning with command and control power structures overseeing neat and tidy standardized production units. Modernism created everything that was big. Economies of scale were the industrial paradigm: mass-production, mass-marketing, mass-consumption and mass-pollution. The steel and glass skyscrapers of the 1970s were a monument to the industrial revolution.

Even as large modern corporations were erecting large modern buildings to house their large modern management practices, architectural writers were identifying a wafting change in the way people were thinking about life and society. Inspired by writers such as the deconstructionist Jacques Derrida, they exposed a coming Postmodern era. The machine was dying; the organic network was taking its place.

In the ultra-consumer 1980s, a deconstruction of the machine began to grow. Big, immutable power structures began ceding to more nimble networks. Buildings and other man-made artifacts gained more variety, more flexibility and more life. A pluralism of technical, aesthetic, ethical and spiritual interests appeared. The business world invented virtual corporations. All kinds of people became free agents, and the Internet exploded onto the scene, evoking references to changes in world commerce more significant than the industrial revolution.

Postmodernism is a return to pluralism from uniformity, where individuals regain their creative autonomy and nonscientific ideas like purpose and values become important once again. Cultural pluralism has led to commercial democracy. A mass of young and creative entrepreneurs have gained access to a commercial arena they would have otherwise been shut out from a decade ago.

Early in the revolution, however, there was an insufferable and e-rational rant about how e-commerce and e-this and e-that would replace the old modern industrial economy (quite e-xhausting and e-xasperating), but the April 2000 market correction humbled the zealots whose dotcom speculations came crashing down. The first act in the New Economy failed to fulfill the hype: the pendulum swung too far. Amazon did not put Barnes and Noble out of business; Walmart, the largest bricks-and-mortar retailer, may yet become the world's largest website.

Ironically, many of the generation of hyper entrepreneurs have found employment from the very people they were plotting to put out of business. Many large modern corporations have subsumed the innovations of the acumen-lacking young pioneers. These monolithic entities are learning to adapt the strengths of economic efficiency with the more nimble and creative thinking of the next generation. *The next wave in the economy is the reconciliation of modern and post-modern ways – a hybrid approach that balances the best of the old and new.*

Building Service Staples, Repeat Business and Residual Income

Back in the early part of the last century, a salesman named King Gillette invented the safety razor. His product consisted of a robust handle that held a replaceable blade. As the now famous story goes, people would not ante up the high price for the razor, so Gillette lowered the price of the razor to well below its manufactured cost and raised the price of the blades. The blades are of course a staple product, one that requires constant replenishing, and the high cost of the razor got buried or amortized within the margin on the blades. Instead of a small number of people making a higher one-time purchase, King changed the situation into one with many people able to make a lifetime of smaller purchases: "give away the razor and sell the blades," as the dictum now goes.

By altering the economics of the initial purchase, staples increase the lifetime value of a customer: the sum of all future profits on products that a customer would purchase in a lifetime discounted for the time-value of money. Since it is a well known marketing truism that it is much easier and less costly to sell to an existing customer than a new one, staples can be a very profitable source of repeat purchases and long-term revenue with much lower sales and marketing costs.

To identify opportunities for designing staple products, it is useful to move from a product focus to a customer focus. A true customer focus does not just mean to include the customer in the design of services and products but to make the customer a focus of the design process. In their *One-to-One* series Don Peppers and Martha Rogers describe customer focus as moving from the idea of selling a smaller number of products to a larger number of customers to selling a larger number of products to a smaller number of customers. This also means a move from trying to capture greater market share to capturing a greater share of individual customer's purchases. There are compelling economics in doing so from reduced selling cost. Once a company has earned the trust of a customer and that company and customer have invested time, energy and money in a relationship, it is simply more convenient to maintain and even expand the scope of the relationship.

Such high-scope customer relationships are perennial. Customers return year after year to consume the staples of the company and to lever the relationship. Such a shift also requires that marketing move from product-focused to values-focused. Core values are ultimately what binds customers to any venture. Once we see that our purpose is to continually create a set of values for a set of customers, we are free to think up other offers. The crux point is how we position ourselves in the minds of our core clients. If we position ourselves as a product or service, we may unwittingly trap ourselves into a narrow view of what our businesses are really about.

In my business, for example, I see my purpose as contributing innovation to professional service entrepreneurs. Although I have increasing levels of consciousness around these ideas, they have always been true for me. Through a somewhat radical series of product shifts, the constants in my life are my two focal points: innovation and entrepreneurs. When I was a product designer, it was true. When I was a project manager, it was true. When I was a venture capitalist, it was true. And now as a writer, speaker and coach, it is true. If I had defined myself according to these limited technicalities, I would not be able to see the transitions from one to the next. My unique contribution (innovation) and core client definition (entrepreneurs) have remained constant through a series of structural changes. Also, many of my customers have followed me through each transition. *By defining our ventures according to our unique contributions and core clients, we are free to design an endless series of products that extend the lifetime value of our client base.*

In speaking of what drives humanity forward, the futurist Barbara Marx Hubbard made the distinction between procreation and co-creation as two expressions of the same underlying creative energy. These energies suffuse the entire human project with its drive towards excellence, legacy, innovation, compassion and the advancement of worthy projects. Procreation is of course the biological driver of physical evolution, that pleasurable activity that supports continuity of our species and the refinement of our internal adaptive responses to the natural environment through successive generations. Co-creation drives cultural evolution, which allows us to create external responses, quicker. When our collaborations work, they seem to be equally pleasurable.

Working with other people to create artifacts is the pleasurable spiritual analog to the natural selection processes working inside of our bodies. Robert Wright, a cultural anthropologist who wrote *Non Zero*, a book depicting the natural synergistic processes within society, draws out an historical comparison between these two kinds of evolutions. He also noted that throughout history, mankind was able to make quantum leaps forward in technological and social innovation only when people were able to work together to bring them about. This "co-labouring" results from the successful breaching of two barriers: the trust barrier and the communication barrier.

Consider a recent striking example described in *Fast Company* magazine and drawn from the new economy: the Linux software platform, the brainchild of Linus Torvalds. Unlike my beloved Macintosh or Windows which are proprietary and closed systems – the source code is not publicly available – the Linux system is completely open and accessible to any one who wishes to access it and refine it. At any given time there are hundreds of volunteer project leaders guiding the work of thousands more volunteer programmers each working on a segment of the code. Such a posse of programmers has breached the trust barrier because they are working solely for the recognition that comes from creating elegant code. No one gains any real property rights, and everyone has equal access to the final product. The software itself is also more trustworthy because there are so many more talented programmers refining it, compared to the relatively small ranks working inside companies for hire on proprietary projects. Linux has resisted the assaults of many strains of virus which have breached other closed systems.

The network of programmers has also broken through the communications barrier by using the Internet and a unique project management scheme. Anyone is free to volunteer refinements and bug-fixes, and the leaders presiding over a section of code decide which are best. Linux is a very interesting prototype of cultural evolution and open-source co-creation: an artifact revolving through several thousand iterations of continual refinement, supported by a community of collaborators working towards the joint expression of elegance.

Collaborative work processes pose an interesting opportunity for creative entrepreneurs: the greatest power may come from giving power away. Linus Torvalds possesses the kind of collaborative power that is the opportunity of future waves of the New Economy. He opened access to the creative process to people outside of his own enterprise and ended up creating an entirely different enterprise based on the free distribution of control and the opportunity to contribute. *Entrepreneurs who overcome the trust and communication barriers to distributive collaboration access the wealth of intellectual and human capital held in the network of their people.*

The Virus in Viral Marketing   **46**
Designing A Core Meme

Quite sometime ago, the evolutionary biologist and computer scientist Richard Dawkins proposed the idea of a "meme." Like its biological analog, the meme is a unit of replication, in this case cultural, rather than physical. Ideas, songs, trademarks, concepts, designs are all memes. They are pieces of culture, artifice that gets easily passed from one person to another. Dawkins suggested and authors Richard Brodie and Robert Wright have elaborated that these memes are the equivalent of a cultural virus. Once the meme gets into your mind a copy stays there while you pass along other copies to other minds. This is the basis of viral marketing.

The original and most famous case of viral marketing was Hotmail, a free email service that eventually became a Microsoft staple bought for US$450M. With Hotmail, someone sends you an email, and at the bottom is a link to the Hotmail website where you can sign up for your own free account. It spread like a virus – geometrically and rapidly. I tell two friends and you tell two friends, and so on, and so on. Such an approach to viral marketing is difficult to duplicate simply because its viral driver was that the email was free. It has now been done. Hotmail was a good meme, in the sense of its rapid spread.

A more substantive approach to meme design and one that does not require giving away your product is devising the core meme. Nike's core meme is "Just Do it." I suspect there are more copies of that meme in the world than Hotmail accounts. That phrase has also probably driven more sales and wealth for Nike than Hotmail has for Microsoft.

The term "viral marketing" was coined by Steve Jurveston, the venture capitalist behind Hotmail. Like many things in the New Economy, viral marketing is not really new.

Email just makes the replication cycle much faster. Still, the basis of viral marketing is the meme.

A good meme, as Brodie points out, is not so much one which is virtuous but one which spreads easily. We can create a good meme in both the virtuous sense and the replication sense by writing an authentic tagline. The tagline connotes what a company is about in language that works for a specific audience. "Just Do It" somehow spoke well about the core Nike ideas of victory and competitive spirit and to what was happening in the athletic world at the time, in a way that caught on. When Nike first launched the phrase, fad diets and sugar pills were losing their favour; and Nike was losing market share to the upstart Reebok. "Just Do It" became the mantra not only for the company's resurgence against Reebok but for people who, deep down, knew that the only way to really lose weight and get fit is to get on with it and do the work (a novel idea from the never-to-be-a-best-selling-book *How to Lose Weight by Exercising and Eating Less!*). The tagline works not because it is a cute phrase but because it struck a chord between what was going on inside Nike and what was going on outside in the world of it customers. It is a pandemic phrase, authentic to both the company and the population of its clients. It brought them together and has held them together.

A good tagline is an effective meme that reflects who I am at the core, in language that works for and attracts my best customers. My customers, staff, allies and prospective customers pass it around. My company is about "innovation", bringing entrepreneurs and their clients more closely together in a relationship that is more meaningful and fulfilling to both. My tagline is "Higher Purpose, Higher Profit". This means "innovation", but, more importantly, it is a phrase that reaches out to my best prospects who identify with the mantra. *A good tagline reflects who we are, attracts the best clients and spreads like a virus.*

Finding a Place in the Community of Conscious Entrepreneurs

The human species recently achieved a population of six billion, well-beyond the theoretical capacity of the natural environment. Fifty years ago, forecasters predicted all manner of strife, an end to food and the beginning of the end of the human time and place. Their argument was that as food supply increases arithmetically, population increases geometrically. Interestingly, widespread famine has not struck and, while some despots and terrorists have taken ardent shots at it, no tyrant has succeeded in destroying the planet. While some areas of the planet still lag, the global family seems to be enjoying improved quality of life most everywhere. Good will and enlightened self-interest live on. Ingenious people answer the calls of desperation, service and opportunity. Humanity continues to engineer itself out of improbable difficulties and impasses. The spirited creative source we all access has moved us into a new enlightenment and has created new opportunities beyond mass imagination.

One thing seems apparent to me: that the forward progress of the world is increasingly less driven by a small number of tyrants and more driven by a collective consciousness – one mind, or what Teilhard de Chardin called the "noosphere." Case in point, I have watched the world's richest man and others try unsuccessfully to dominate one of the most powerful recent social inventions – the Internet, which has become the technical vehicle of common consciousness. Despite some current and historical disruptions of global peace, it seems that the days where a small number of people can decide the fates and fortunes of everyone else are largely behind us. Even severe acts of terrorism are triggering widespread initiatives to preserve democracy, freedom and opportunity. Anyone can gain knowledge, anyone can access resources and anyone can innovate. This age of democracy has become the age of enterprise and the age of the entrepreneur.

Irrespective of size and scope, each entrepreneur has an important part in the powerful play of making the world work better for everyone. I still remember the day I realized I was not set to become Bill Gates. As a young person, I bought into the narrow and grandiose view of what innovation and business was all about. But, between self-aggrandizement and fatalistic resignation lies many paths and opportunities to live a meaningful life and contribute to our people and planet. It is not so much about domination and sheer size, but realizing my own personal fulfillment in the service of others: my friends, family, customers and allies. We are held together by a philosophy of service and a need to contribute. Impact is difficult to measure and perhaps the futile game of the ego anyway. We can never really know the full ramifications of some small and seemingly inconsequential act of generosity and kindness that we might make. But we can enjoy the process and have faith that despite the invisibility of the impact of many of our contributions, we have made a difference. Our contributions strengthen the lives of people close to us, who in turn use that strength to improve the lot of those around them. In very little time, a single honourable deed can shift the planet.

In the end, we matter not because we can prove that we do, but because we are members of a powerful collective consciousness that continues to shape the experiences of all of us, largely for the better. We are alive and we have a contribution to make to the larger reality that will soon record us into the oblivion of its history. If we are lucky, we might become a foot note in the appendix of an out-of-print book, chronicling the most important events that ever happened. In the face of this, our roles may simply be to enjoy life, make our contributions and release any of the more archaic drives towards dominance, fame and even legacy. Live big today and then live even bigger tomorrow.

Putting More Soul into Relationships with Clients

An article in *Forbes* magazine introduced the idea of a "cult brand", citing the Mazda Miata, Apple Computer and Harley Davidson, as examples of companies who have garnered an overwhelmingly tenacious and enthusiastic client base. It would be easy to add Starbucks to the list of companies whose customers are so passionate about the company that they regularly line up to pay premium prices for its offerings. Cult brands engender lucrative long-term relationships that weather the occasional storms of economic recession, intensifying competition and management error.

The glue that binds people to an enterprise, whether they are client, investor or employee is loyalty. Many people have an innate need to be a part of something. This is why it is so compelling for human beings to bond themselves together in all forms of organizations. Being a member of a customer community is no different. The people who drive Harley Davidson motorcycles, like the people who use Macintosh computers or drink Starbucks coffee are members of a social group that share a somewhat common language and culture. It means something to drive a Harley or use a Mac or have a cup of Starbucks. The people who partake of such experiences are connected in some way to a deeper reality, surrounding the companies. They have bought into more than a product.

Loyalty has its roots in Latin, meaning "legal", suggesting that a binding agreement is in place between client and company and that each remains true to the implied obligations: the company agrees to live up to what it stands for, and the client agrees to remain a devoted patron. In current language, the word means to be faithful, to be full of faith or to keep the faith. For me, faith comes down to issues of core beliefs and core values. From this perspective, loyalty is the bond formed in the soulful connection between customer and company. That bond is the contract that endures. Deep bonds, like those formed amongst marriage partners or long-standing friends reflect an enmeshing of value systems that are not transactional but spiritual. Parties to those sort of meaningful relationships are more likely to describe their partners as soulmates. In business, loyalty is not so much about great products, dazzling service and cool marketing. If it was about these qualities, then clients would be gone the moment competitors offered more. Loyalty is a spiritual connection.

One company I am loyal to is Ventura, California's Patagonia. Patagonia makes clothing for all kinds of challenging outdoor pursuits: climbing, skiing, surfing, white water kayaking and fishing. That fact, in itself, is unremarkable. What is remarkable is the fanatic-like following of "Patagoniacs" and the consistently high prices and margins. Patagonia is consistently the most expensive supplier in the outdoor industry. They do not try to be mass-market leaders, rather they limit the distribution of their products. They are hard to get.

The clothing itself, while being as good or better than other outdoor clothing suppliers, is not why I buy. I am spiritually connected to the environmental world view of the company. They appear committed to the ideal of an enduring natural environment and to making versatile and enduring products that contribute to solving the environmental crisis. The concept of "endurance" is the soul that binds me to the company, just as the concepts of "tradition", "community" and "innovation" are the souls that bind customers to Harley Davidson, Starbucks and Apple, respectively. *When a company consistently lives up to the promise of the values implied by its world view, the company earns the loyalty of its high value customers, repeat business, forgiveness for its errors and protection from the lure of competitors.*

The emerging integrative health model proposes that mind and body are intimately connected and practitioners must treat people as whole systems. Sitting in the overlap between the mental and physical valences of human existence and the traditions of Western allopathic medicine and Eastern mysticism, is the full range of emotional experience. In the Chinese tradition, for example, the liver stores the emotion of anger. I would have dismissed this notion prior to a detoxification cleanse of my liver. For three days a miserable stream of hate poured out from me as I rid my body of the many angry memories I had suppressed over the years. Toxins are not just the physical poisons my liver accumulates from the environment, they are also the negative emotional patterns I store there.

People literally wear their stress in various parts of their bodies. It is not unusual for people who do not want to look at certain issues in their lives to develop problems with their sight, for people who think they must carry the problems of the world on their own shoulders to develop back or neck strain or for people who are suppressing their creativity or abundance to develop issues in their reproductive areas. When I am under a certain kind of stress, I clench my jaw, sometimes to the point that I cannot chew. That means that I am afraid to let go of something, like a dog on a bone.

I have been working on this with a holistic dentist named Bill Cryderman. Part of my problem is biomechanical. The seating of my lower jaw into my upper jaw is misaligned in all three dimensions. Bill knows that correcting my bite, the interface between my teeth and the action of my jaw are body-side issues that will not eliminate the tension of the muscles in the temporal mandibular joint. The mind-side comes from understanding and releasing some deep-seated emotions.

In my almost therapeutic discussions with Bill, I have begun to identify the emotional part of the issue that comes from my family history and how that history has set forth some relationship patterns. I have a high need for connection. In times of apparent or anticipated scarcity, I am sensitive to rejection and vulnerable to the fear of loss. When this fear is active, my reaction is to hold on to what I have. One such period is usually December and the Christmas season. This is a naturally slow season for business; my revenues thin and my expenditures rise for the gift-giving season. The issue has something to do with my parent's divorce when I was eleven. My father left that Christmas. My father leaving was the first major experience of loss I had as a young person. Prior to that, I had been an active and successful artist. When my father left home, I stopped my primary mode of expression, deciding not to express anything but to keep everything inside, where no one could take it away.

I am dogmatic and tend to push myself on people when I am in a place of scarcity. I can actually manufacture rejection by being dogmatic and pushing good prospective clients away. Failing then to create cashflow leads to more scarcity and the risk of pushing the next prospect away. At some point during this downward spiral, I will begin to feel the fear of loss rise and my jaw will begin to stiffen. My jaw stress has now become a great barometer for scarcity. Mounting jaw stress now reminds me to look for new opportunities and to reconnect with the oneness of the universe, abundance and the idea that the right people are out there and know they need me. At that point I return to life as an artist, feeling safe to express what I have. Such emotional expression, as it turns out, is very attractive and does not lead to either rejection or loss, but acceptance and gain. *We can solve sometimes serious business problems by learning to listen to and interpret the personal feedback our physical bodies are giving us.*

A Living Legacy   50
Working to Make the World Better for Future Generations

I recently discovered that I am going to die. May be not now, or
soon, but someday, and for some of us that day is sooner than we
ever would have thought. This is not trite. Up until recently, I
had successfully hidden the knowledge of my mortality
underneath a thick cloak of intellectual justification and
suppressed fear. I knew, of course, that I was going to die; I just
never accepted that it was really true.

I think we are entrepreneurs precisely because of our
relationships with death (and taxes for that matter). Decades
of writing have cited entrepreneurship as the process of
building something and creating some kind of durable legacy.
Perhaps entrepreneurs have the most unresolved feelings about
death and the greatest need to leave something of themselves
behind. Through a legacy we become immortal. Richard
Dawkins, following along in the Darwinian world view, wrote
a seminal piece called *The Selfish Gene*. He believed, that
while our bodies may be ephemeral packages that come and go,
our genes live on in the bodies of our children, in a sort of genetic
immortality. Some level of our programming ensures that we
take actions to assure the viability of our progeny. And,
progeny need not be biological but cultural. Architects 500 years
ago, authors of the great European cathedrals, never lived to
see their projects completed. The cathedrals are still standing,
having withstood wars, indifference and acid rain. But despite
their duration, all material monuments eventually disin-
tegrate.

If most material legacies eventually fade, what will
live on past our scheduled deaths? Probably not some great
piece of prose, or some "killer app", or a great negotiation or a
profoundly worded mission statement. These are present
moment, technical achievements. Still, being a conscious
entrepreneur is at least as spiritual as it is technical. And the

spiritual realm exists because of death. If death did not exist, we would not need to wonder what happened afterward. We would not have to develop belief systems and faith. There might even be no urgency to create.

Over ten years ago, I witnessed the funeral of Bill March, a great climber and mentor. Then, I presided over the funeral of another climber, one of my best friends, Karl Nagy. Both men led daring lives and were struck down in their prime, long before either would have expected it. It seems that both had managed to touch an incredibly large number of people during their short tenure, with most of whom showing up at the funeral services.

Of all the types of prosperity that exist, be it information, possessions, fame or fortune, it seems to me that the most poignant and lasting legacy is the impact we have on the people around us. Residual contribution seems to be the ultimate kind of wealth. The lasting impact we have on our people and planet may even be what we take with us, as we leave this life. How do we finally measure the value of our contributions? One way is by the people we leave behind, who would cancel their plans, travel from afar and do anything it takes to come to our funerals and say good-bye.

We all stand on the shoulders of giants who went before. As we make the most of this life, we are really taking our place within a rich historical, social network of goodwill. We live now, taking for granted the invisible contributions and gifts of those who strived and struggled and went before. Future generations will enjoy the fruits of our mutual labours. Today we are making the world better just as future generations have done for us. *Our real legacy is the love we leave behind when we are gone: a world that works better not just for our friends and family, but for everyone who has yet to be born. That is the ultimate community.*

Part III: Elegance
Moving Forward with Grace

Creating Power and Higher Momentum

Finding the Natural Cadence of Growth

There are two kinds of runners: sprinters and distance runners. When I was young, I was a sprinter. I liked going fast, and I cared little for endurance. As I grew older, I continued to do everything fast. When I became an entrepreneur I did that fast too. It was easy for me to think that this was the only way to achieve success – all the great entrepreneurs I read about, they went fast too. Everything is done on Internet time, a business has an 8 week launch window and if we do not move fast, we are all told, someone else will get there first. My problem with speed in business was that the faster I went, the less I enjoyed the process. I tripped up more than I needed to, I was constantly out of balance and wildly out of my comfort zone. It was difficult, miserable and frequently impoverishing. Any business I started, did not last.

When I took up distance running, I hired a coach to train me. Grant Molyneux, my "vitality coach", taught me a completely different way to train, and run based on finding and staying just at the edge of comfort and balance were performance increases and enjoyment are optimal. I had thought that to grow, as a runner or an entrepreneur, I needed to be wildly outside of my comfort zone, speeding along with a "no pain, no gain" mentality. Grant has taught me that a comfort zone needs to be stretched but not torn. When I first met Grant he was giving a breakfast speech to a bunch of fitness-minded professionals. The first thing I noticed was his inclusion of bacon for breakfast. I thought that any fitness plan that included bacon was a good fitness plan, so I joined up.

Of course, I had been approaching distance running as a sprinter, going out and running as fast as I could until I puked or killed my knees. My first training session with Grant consisted of a 45 minute walk with a five minute run in between. He told me to slow my pace and reduce my cadence any time I felt discomfort in my body: a twinge in the knee, an uncomfortable breath, anything. So I backed off, then slowly increased my pace, backed off again at the sign of pain, then increased my pace, and so on. In no time I was running, in total comfort and balance for forty-five minutes, and I was able to complete my first distance race. While it was only ten kilometres and it was not particularly quick, it was considerably longer than the hundred meter dashes to which I was accustomed. I have found my natural and optimum cadence, which has grown gracefully over time.

I learned this same lesson about pacing from several mountain guides. I hired one to teach my climbing partners and I some advanced mountaineering and safety techniques and was quite shocked to learn that we were to spend the first half of the first day learning to walk. Of course, I resisted the notion, thinking full well I knew how to walk, but as I watched the guide, my view expanded. I had heard the axiom-cliché – walk before you run. I never really embraced it until that day. It turns out, quite counter-intuitively, that it is faster and takes less energy to take many small steps than fewer larger ones. The guide taught us to walk deliberately, to anticipate each step within the context of a larger view of the landscape ahead. Rather than bolt forward and burnout, we learned to pace ourselves and find our optimum cadence. We enjoyed the process and summit more.

I have applied these lessons to my business. *It is often more enjoyable, faster and more efficient to build a business with many smaller steps than to bolt forward and burnout with fewer larger and more strenuous steps.* I have released my more grandiose visions. I have slowed down, caught my breath and found my own natural and optimum cadence. I have learned to actually enjoy the process of moving with comfort and balance.

Two of my wisest leadership mentors need only two hands to count their years of passage on this earth. Perhaps those of you who have children have marveled at the precocious moments of your child's utter brilliance. Like many parents, I sometimes like to think that mine were the first ever progeny to concoct a stunning aesthetic masterpiece, to fashion a witty outlook on the matter of life purpose or to wrestle out some bold athletic monument. Their achievements inspire me.

Inside each new child there seems to lie a perfect shiny promise of some untold greatness largely unspoiled by the vagaries of family, culture and society. Such external influences seem to be actively working to vanquish their innate unique character and reduce them to some mediocre standard, tolerable only by the most insecure and eldest of our society. Most children eventually burst forth in direct proportion to the severity of any oppressive forces that has sought or seeks to undermine their full expression. If they do not rise above their wounds, then their spirits slowly die, and the bodies of their unfulfilled gifts wither away into the tragic dust of important lives lost forever.

Every child has some wounds. These might not be the sting of damaged flesh but instead the emotional scarring of a world not fully prepared to understand the nuances of a young life attempting to flower itself open to it. When our children are young, we are their world. Despite our longing to bring perfect beings gracefully into full fruition, we do not respond with perfect grace to their every need. We ourselves were young once. We have our own wounds and unfulfilled needs. Many of us carry the impossible banners of idyllic family values and the images of perfect hero-parents emblazoned onto our collective child-rearing psyche. We are imperfect parents, bringing imperfect little people into the world. It is our scars and history that make each of us so interesting and unique.

Years ago, when my first-borne son was barely able to walk, my consciousness was full of other concerns. I had made little space for his new creative intrusion. He disrupted a life I had fought hard to keep free of burden and chaos. His arrival prompted a new world of doubts and challenges. For the first years of his life, I pretended not to be a father. This was the easiest thing to do, and a skill I had perfected prior to needing it by watching my own. My dad was uneasy with children and had a parenting style I did not initially appreciate. I thought he liked the idea of having children more than actually having them. Perhaps it was some drive towards a legacy and the sense of family he never had. Maybe it was an opportunity to pass on the mantle of clanship without the inconvenience of real feelings or intimacy. Of course, these are really judgments best made about myself. Fatherhood fit me like a hair shirt, its itch a constant reminder of my own deficient paternity.

I still remember the day I became a "real" father. I was walking with my barely verbal, barely mobile young son, when he looked up at me with profound disappointment, as if to say, "Get your shit together; I need a father." I heard that painful message loudly and clearly.

Perhaps it is true that our weakest moments owe some quiet homage to an unbroken chain of family members who went before. It could be that some mysterious genetic codes force us into repeating the sins of our ancestors. Perhaps we are taught by well-meaning parents and a well-meaning society how we ought to be and how we ought to behave, and then we unconsciously accept the contract. And perhaps these are just lame excuses. I found my courage in the eyes of an inspired two-year old who made a different choice and broke a cycle that was not working for him. *Real leadership comes from people who are clear about what they want and find the courage inside to stand up and ask for it.*

At the tender age of eighteen, I fell under the spell of the mountains and taught myself to rock climb. My ascent into climbing was not unlike my ascent into entrepreneurship: my enthusiasm was matched only by my lack of skill and judgment. This meant, among other things, that I found myself in frequent adventures. The word "adventures" is a euphemism used by "adventurers" to describe any situation where they get lost, off-route or in any other kind of interesting trouble.

The route I chose for my first BIG adventure was a cliff first climbed in the late '50s; so I began the enterprise completely underestimating the severity of the hazards and challenges I would find on route. Most of the climbing went surprisingly well, bolstering my naive confidence. Then, standing on a small ledge with the man who would hold my rope should I fall, I scanned the last fifty meters to the top of the cliff. I had been following the guide book all day, but I could not make any sense out of the description of the last pitch. There was a cavernous slot of parallel-sided walls on my left and a steep, blank-looking slab of rock to my right. I spotted a metal piton far out on the right side. I could not see or imagine a route to the left into the improbable cave, so I assumed that was the way.

The anchors at our tiny stance were small, corroded spikes of iron bashed uneasily into the soft limestone. It was all I could do to scratch my way out from there to the peg, only to find out it was bent over and almost rusted-through. I clipped my rope into it anyway, hoping for some vague comfort. From there it seemed like I was off route, but I could not fathom how to reverse what I had just done. So I retreated vertically up the climb, hoping, instead, that I would find a way through the maze to the top. I climbed for another thirty meters without finding any anchors for my useless rope. I then found myself stuck halfway up a fifteen foot slab of featureless rock, below a spacious ledge, with a clear and easy traverse back left to what I had, by now, figured out was the proper route.

All that separated me from safety was a five foot stretch of rock beyond the reach of my fingers. I could not see a way to go up, and climbing down, what I had barely climbed up, was not an option either. So I just stood there, getting gripped with fear. I had my left foot placed on a small nubbin of rock, with two fingers of my left hand snagged on a tiny seam. I rested my other foot and hand on mirror-smooth rock to my right, to stay in balance. I stared hopelessly through my outstretched legs into the void below, only to see my redundant rope flap aimlessly in the wind. I looked down at my partner some thirty meters below on the ledge, at the rusty anchors between us and then down at the ground for the first time that day. Somehow I had not noticed that we had accumulated three hundred meters of dead vertical air between the ground and my precariously planted feet. The gravity of the situation set in, and I considered the possibility of death for the first time in my life. I began to sweat, placing unwelcome lubricant between the callouses of my fingers and the crystals of rock on which they were tenuously stuck. My feet started to vibrate.

I was on the verge of peeling off, when I recall making the choice to live. I looked down at my one good foot and saw a tiny gash only two inches higher. I moved my foot to that spot and stood up. My angle of view changed just enough that I saw a small crystal for my right index finger and other small features which I quickly knit into a viable escape path. I rehearsed the moves once in my head, and, with a rush of calm, I flowed up to the large ledge and easily on to the summit.

Faced with their own demise, people show amazing abilities to find solutions. Breaching an impasse, whether in the wilds of nature or in business, is sometimes just a matter of moving tiny steps forward, steps that can radically alter the landscape of possibilities.

Capturing the Nature and Soul of a New Kind of Enterprise

In 1995, Bill Gates declared that the Internet was a fad. Arguably the world's greatest entrepreneur and visionary failed to acknowledge one of the most important developments of the Twentieth Century and the early part of the New Millennium. To me, apart from being funny, this marked the end of the traditional "strategic planning" movement.

At its best, strategic planning sought to guide an organization through to its highest and best. At its worst, it became an infamous process marshaled by a handful of senior managers, wearing ugly golf shirts at a frivolous off-site retreat. They would spend their time there rationally defining the mission of the firm in the form of motherhood statements about outstanding value to customers, high quality and extraordinary return to shareholders, developing a lofty vision by doing some kind of strength-weakness-opportunity-threat analysis and then writing a "plan" to fulfill the vision. Once the future was "forged", they would congratulate themselves and return to the trenches to drive the new vision down through the rank and file in true command and control style, to the mantra, "Get it right the first time." This snuffed the creative spirits of the staff and made it terrifying to fail.

Traditional planning is top-down, linear and sequential: a design-build-sell model. This way seemed right in the prosperous postwar years, when consumer spending power was increasing and supply was limited in both volume and variety. People would buy anything. Forty years later, when supply and variety had increased with the discriminating tastes of the market, customers became unwilling to buy just anything. Ted Levitt, Phil Kotler and other academics invented the "marketing concept", to reflect the shift in power from maker to buyer. The notion was to build something that someone wants, a sell-design-build model. This seemed logical, but customers are not; they rarely know what they want. Nobody initially wanted the telephone, the computer or the Internet. Both the design-build-sell model and the sell-design-build model fail to balance the whims of customers and the novelty of makers. They are still linear, rational, "get it right the first time" models.

Organic planning is more natural, with several kinds of development activities done in parallel: sell-sell-build-design-build-design-sell-design-build-build-sell or whatever combination seems to fit the innovation. The Internet, for example, is an organic phenomenon. Nobody really knows for sure how important it is, where it is going or how to get it right the first time. It is neither linear nor rational.

Nature has no precedent for "getting it right the first time." There are innovations, especially in a quickly moving, unpredictable economy, that we cannot "theory" ourselves through. As Tom Peters pointed out: "Nothing really interesting was ever done right even the hundredth time." Successful organisms become successful by constantly changing over many generations, and successful business organizations thrive over time through creative iterations of selling, building and designing. Imagine the absurdity of a traditional strategic planning committee trying to plan something as complex and beautiful as a human body.

All organic forms result from two forces – the internal coding present in their DNA and their adaptations to a constantly changing external environment. Organic planning respects both coding and adaptation. Coding comes from issues of soul: who we are, why we exist, what we value, what we have to offer and what we are here to contribute. Adaptation comes from how we make it work for the people we serve in the context of constantly shifting business environment. *An organic planning process unfolds with a fluid and conscious enterprise, balancing the enduring character of its purpose and values with the continuously evolving environment of its technologies, customers and competitors.*

Marshall McLuhan said, "If it works, it's obsolete." In business, obsolescence means stale products, boring stories, indifferent selling, stressful organizations and looming financial scarcity: the price for not keeping pace with change. Every business detail is a result of decisions we make. We make every decision based on certain assumptions and "facts." Over time, these change. Thus a decision that was good in the past may not be good for the future. There are four things that always change.

The first three are field-dependent: customers, technology and competitors. Society and culture are fluid organic influences on people. Their needs and tastes evolve and they grow dissatisfied and bored. Every day, new information, new discoveries and new science appear to create new technical opportunities. And these are available to many companies who use them to change their offerings and the other parts of their business structure. These factors are environmental, external to our businesses and largely beyond our control. They are out there. The best we can do is pay attention, accept reality and respond proactively: change our businesses before we are forced to by dissatisfied customers, the latest technology or aggressive competitors. Unlike "planned obsolescence", invented postwar by the famous car designer Harley Earle, author of tail fins and tail lights that made cars look like jet airplanes, this is not change for the sake of change. This is about making the right change at the right time and controlling what we can control.

The fourth factor that always changes but is not field-dependent is the personality, character and self-knowledge of the entrepreneur. An overlooked source of innovation is how well we know ourselves. It's not what we know that controls us , it is often what we do not know. At any one time, we are conscious of only a small portion of what we really "know." Because our unconscious is a deep well, there is endless learning available. This is under our control. We can become more conscious of why we are in business, our values, passion and what we stand for. These are important components of a good business and they reside inside of us.

Complete business intelligence requires both an external and internal awareness. Great entrepreneurs are known for their creativity, tenacity, resourcefulness, courage and resilience. They are also introspective and seek to discover their own deep truth about their internal strengths and weaknesses. They know who they are, why they are alive and what difference they intend to make. They build their businesses to respect these values, and their businesses work better because of it.

Investment in personal development is a powerful source of business profit. What we learn about ourselves completes the picture of what we learn about customers, technology and competitors. Becoming more conscious of our natural strengths and the self-sabotaging patterns that erode our potential is a great source of new opportunities for productive change and meaningful expression.

As our ventures grow, they progress through an endless series of phases that reflect our changing awareness of forces inside and outside the venture. Each successful phase is marked by a period of adaptation, stagnation and obsolescence. New business models come and go in a repeating cycle of growth spurts and plateaus, like an endless escalator upwards. Personal transformation, growth and development often precede their business analogs. *No matter how successful we get, the conditions upon which we base our success are sure to change: there is always somewhere to go, something to learn and some improvement to make in the continual process of personal and business evolution.*

Moving Towards a Compassionate Definition of Integrity

The entrepreneurial scholar Ed McMullan once proposed that perhaps the greatest entrepreneurial trait was a high tolerance for ambiguity. This is perhaps the demarcation between people who work for a business and people who build them. Indeed, many people quite reasonably choose employment because of the regularity and certainty of pay checks, while the entrepreneurs learn to deal with a myriad of uncertainties. Not that employees face no uncertainty, but the entrepreneurial problem, in the strictest sense, is a dialog about the essential viability of the entire enterprise: "What do customers really want?", "How can we make this technology work?", "Will our finances hold until operating cash flows kick in?", "Is this the best opportunity?", "Will we be able to hire any decent people?", "Will we be able to make payroll this month?", "Are we going to be able to win that bid?", "Is a stronger competitor going to arrive?", "Is this going to work?"

Integrity is an important concept amongst service providers. The companies that possess it earn the loyalty and trust of a valuable base of customers who will see the company through all of its heady growth. The most frequently used definition of integrity I have heard is that of "keeping our word." The questions now for entrepreneurs are: how does one keeps one's word in a volatile environment of ambiguity?, and, what kind of word ought we give?

I once saw a movie where the protagonist-hero says to the damsel-in-distress, "I never make a promise I can't keep." Most people would agree that within that phrase lies the purest form of integrity – the ultimate noble and romantic definition of this precious concept. It also, unfortunately, promotes a risk aversion that undermines a tolerance of ambiguity. Why is this so? If we only make promises we know we can keep, we never make any bold promises we are unsure about whether we can keep. The consequence is we commit only to what we know will work. As entrepreneurs this is simply not a viable approach to integrity or enterprise. It sets up an unrealistic set of expectations. Either we play small and make no bold offers, or we make bold offers and hate ourselves for failing to deliver on them.

An experimental mindset is a more compassionate and practical approach to the matter of both enterprise and integrity. The fundamental commitment is, "I am making this work; I may not know how right now, but I am dedicating myself to do whatever it takes to make my contribution to the people I care most about." The experimental approach means we make a multitude of smaller trials and promises to create a viable design. We make promises, and we keep promises, then as the future unfolds, we renegotiate as needed.

Most great achievements are the results of bold commitments. Early in the previous century, the Scottish explorer W.H. Murray, in answering the critics of his early expedition to an unclimbed Mt. Everest, said, "...when one truly commits oneself, then Providence moves too...". We deal with an ambiguous future by taking tiny steps forward and being prepared to change our approach in real time. Making rigid promises about what the future will look like only sets us up for failure. Thus, we can commit to our ventures without the requirement of knowing how we will keep our promise. *The strength of our convictions and the power of our forward progress reveal the secrets to our future success, many of which are unknowable at the time of commitment.* This is the kind of integrity that applies to the "process" of getting results, not just the "result" itself. The act of giving our word is a pure act quite separate from the all the methods of keeping it. Boldness in an environment of ambiguity may be the only viable way to maintain the spirit of integrity.

In the frontier days before the Internet and wireless technologies, Nortel, or Northern Telecom as it was known, had developed a program development protocol it called the "gating process." The process leveraged the creative resources of the company by providing a framework for the research, development, evaluation and selection of new product ideas. A gate is a formal decision point. An interdisciplinary panel would review the merits of the potential innovation against a set of criteria appropriate for its phase of development. People from manufacturing, engineering, sales, marketing, customer service, procurement, finance, accounting, quality control and all the other myriad of groups in the company, each of whom viewing feasibility from their own perspective, decided which ideas could move forward to the next level and which ones would be shelved.

Successful ideas moved through a process of increasingly committed phases of development, each capped by a formal go/no go point. The innovator had to earn the right to move forward and receive the resources they needed for research and development on the path to a successful marketing program. A typical idea would start with some basic market and technical research. If the opportunity appeared viable, the idea would proceed to more detailed user studies, prototyping and simulations. Prototypes, working from the technical and human perspective, would proceed to a market test. The company would manufacture a small batch of the product and take it into a live retail test. If consumers liked the product at a given price-point and the underlying economics of the production process were sound, the company would launch full-scale production, developing the millions of dollars worth of equipment and support to make and sell the product at volume. The final successful program would run for a number of years at a good margin, allowing the company to recoup its large investment in program development and make a nice return to its shareholders.

I suspect that much of the trouble with failing projects and ventures is a lack of disciplined innovation. Many ideas move forward, under the panic and illusion of a fast-moving opportunity window, when they have not earned the right to do so. Then they flounder.

The process and procedures for ramping up and rolling out manufactured products are less complicated and less sophisticated than information businesses or softer services. Manufacturing companies build and then turn on a profit-making machine. Service providers leverage their time.

Consider the case of a successful local author, speaker and trainer. This person pays the price of a long apprenticeship, works hard to develop a skill set, a unique point of view and some experience and then earns the right to publish a great book on this subject. The book becomes a bestseller and the entrepreneur becomes adept at finding high-margin clients and delivering great training programs which earn full marks, full fees and repeat business. The founder then hits full capacity, cannot serve any more clients and has earned the right to recruit and train another trainer. The original entrepreneur, who had been relying on the force of his personality, figures out how to assist someone else to independently repeat the client recruiting and satisfying process. When the second trainer successfully passes the gate of being able to repeat the process on his or her own, the founder earns the right to prototype the recruiting tools and open up a branch office in another city. The lead entrepreneur proves that the business can successfully recruit, train and manage a satellite office and then earns the right to duplicate their model geographically and sustain forward momentum. *Service providers can leverage their time by methodically building a foundation for increasingly valuable phases of growth.*

"Burger" is a term from Internet vernacular that describes a company designed from the start to "flip." A flip scenario is one where the founders aim to exit quickly by selling the company to a larger company or taking the company public. The motive behind a flip is usually a rapid gain in wealth, and while the founders of such enterprises may well create value for some group of customers or investors, their focus is not long-term. This short-term and often shortsighted approach fits with the notion of "Internet time" and the generally acknowledged trend of rapid change in society and technology – what has now become a cult of speed.

Such speed stands in marked contrast to my frequent and profound experiences of nature. I recently discovered a remote mountain valley deep in the recesses of the Ghost river area in Alberta. Walking through huge limestone cliffs, cut from thousands of years of the action by the river, I was struck by the contrast of business speed versus geological speed. Nature endures. Surely, there is constant change in nature – experimentation, adaptation and sometimes even violent, sudden change – but there is still an essential quality that seems to last throughout a multitude of seasons. Many businesses caught up in the ephemeral cult of speed may be isolating themselves from the natural rhythm and cadence of the planet and artificially hastening the demise of their enterprises.

As a person spending considerable time in the outdoors, I have come to appreciate the design of outdoor garments, and the different philosophies of the companies that makes them. Patagonia and The North Face are typical suppliers from the outdoor industry which both make excellent clothing for the most demanding physical environments. These two fine companies have historically led the outdoor market and industry. Each has taken a very different growth path.

The North Face is an adventurous company that has pursued what seems to me to be the cult of speed and a path of insatiable growth. This has meant continually broadening their product line, broadening the range of outdoor pursuits they equip for and broadening their distribution scope. To achieve this level of growth they have expanded their use of energy and materials, the amount of pollution they create and the number of stores they sell through. They started trading their stock publicly and eventually found their way into lower margin mass-merchants. To maintain a rapid and accelerating pace of growth, they risk outgrowing their niche and losing their brand cache as it becomes all too common. Unlike other growth companies like Starbucks, The North Face does not appear to me to be growing upon a clear set of values, in a well-defined high-value market space.

Patagonia, despite its many growth pains along the way, has thrived by maintaining its niche. Founded by Yvon Chouinard, who would split his year between making gear and traveling around surfing and climbing, the company has from the start blended forward progress with a commitment to balance, lifestyle and environmental design: "You can't do business on a dead planet." The company sits upon a clear environmental platform: they limit the number of products they make and stores that sell them, fund environmental activism, deploy enduring materials and designs, promote vision stretching out one hundred years (like the Iroquois notion of planning seven generations ahead) and pioneer processes like organic cotton and jackets made out of used pop bottles.

Rapid progress can be good for people and the planet but growth for the sake of growth is the same destructive strategy used by a cancer cell. *A sustainable growth company maintains a strong brand, a sweeping long-term vision, high margins and a loyal customer base assuring that the business will endure well past the death of its founder.*

Celebrating Opportunity When it Comes

When I was six years old, I went exploring down the Lake of the Woods with my uncle Bob. The lake is a complicated system of channels and islands anchored by the small town he grew up in. From a lifetime of exploring its reaches, he knew his way around the maze of big terrain. Hours into this trip, I spotted an old derelict boat, wrecked on the shore of some small, unnamed island. I wanted to see it, so at five foot six and unable to see over the rail to the inside, he tossed me up into the relic. As I was flying over the rail, I saw my small body heading right into the heart of huge nest of wasps – a bell-shaped castle of gray papery walls. The next thing I remember, I was in two feet of water, shielded by my uncle who was being attacked by the petulant swarm of angry wasps. I did not suffer a single sting. This was the sort of thing that always seemed to happen to my uncle. Tragedy and pain were prices he often paid for a great adventure.

Having survived so many epics, my uncle Bob became known for his art of story telling. Despite all of the tragedy he suffered in his life – he was short and always in fights, his wife died at a very young age, he lost a child and died, himself, prematurely of cancer – he always managed to put a positive spin on life. Tragedy was fodder for the tales of things that happened in the war, things that happened while working on the trains or things that happened when he was out fishin'. He managed to embellish his stories in such a way that, each time he told them, they were always fresh and new. He was also well known for his boisterous celebrations at the Royal Canadian Legion, a drinking establishment frequented by war veterans. When anything even remotely good happened to him, he would go down to the Legion and ring the bell, signaling his intent to buy the house a round of drinks – and he was always ringing the bell. Not only did he have the fastest wallet in town, he was always looking for any excuse to celebrate; the invention of such became his notable skill. In the great adventure of his life, he seemed to be a magnet for tragedy and travail, but he could find the good in everything. He was always happy. He always lived the big adventure.

Henry Ford suggested that many people fail to see opportunity because it comes disguised as hard work. There are many more opportunities than we choose to see. *We sometimes fail to see opportunity because it comes disguised as something uncomfortable or terrifying or tragic and not as something packaged with a warm invitation and an obvious welcome.* Shrouded by fear, these situations are easy to avoid. They look not like a chance for a good time, but for misery and mire.

Life is always happening all around us. Things happen. We might judge some events as bad or negative and others as good or positive. The Buddhists say that situations are essentially empty; they are inherently neither good nor bad, they just exist. We decide if something is good or bad by whether we focus on its loss or gain, whether it presents a threat or an opportunity and whether we place a negative or positive perspective around it. Every situation offers some opportunity to create something worthwhile. But it is a place we must believe in before we see.

I think that our greatest opportunities lie in the areas in which we are most wounded or afraid. For my uncle Bob, these were always about some major setback. The lesson of his life to me was: "Where there is setback, there is opportunity for great adventure." That way of living requires great courage and an act of faith – in his case, the belief that there is good in everything. There is no such thing as tragedy from this perspective. While I am sad that he is gone, I am glad for the inspiration of his life: he was a short man that stood tall.

On the Path of Faith   60
Moving Through Three Phases of Growing Trust

When I started ice climbing almost twenty years ago, an old guide gave me the old saw that "there are old climbers and bold climbers, but no old, bold climbers." I have followed this well-worn advice to achieve a safe and successful career in the mountains (safe and successful being synonymous).

Safety is not easy. Most ice climbs form in gullies at the base of large bowls of accumulated snow, making avalanches by far the gravest objective hazards we face as ice climbers. In the early days, I was largely ignorant of this hazard. I knew that people died ice climbing, but, fortunately, I was still an immortal. Every time I went out, I came back; therefore, I was safe. The first phase of any venture is often marked by this kind of bold hope or blind faith: the pure enthusiasm we have for something new can blind us to its risks and perils. The opening overtures of a new business are often like this, with the participants residing in an optimistic, stuporous fantasy world. Everything is perfect at the start of any new enterprise; nothing has yet happened to challenge our enthusiasm.

At some point in the process, something invariably happens to trigger a crisis of faith. Phase II on my path of ice climbing started when I took an avalanche course. From then on, every ice climb was suspect. I was nervous even on slopes that rarely if ever slide. I became frightened and disillusioned. I lost my motivation and my zeal to climb. I even quit for a time.

It is entertaining to observe groups of people entering this phase of a relationship or venture. Something happens to trigger the dissatisfaction, based solely an an unstated expectation that never materializes. Whether it is a romantic relationship, a business partnership or a client-vendor situation, at this point the honeymoon is over, the easy bliss fades and the participants reveal their "evil" shadow sides.

In the ensuing power struggles, self-interest and fear begin to subsume the sense of possibility and passion that marked the start of the enterprise. This is particularly true of naturally optimistic entrepreneurs who see their trust erode with episode after episode of tragedy. What is really going on is a transformation of consciousness. Fantasy and exuberance established the tone of the first phase and obscured the real risks of the venture and the dark sides of its participants. People wake up in this second phase, sometimes rudely, and the hope they had vapourizes, for a time.

The final phase of trust building is the discovery of real faith and a fully-bloomed consciousness of real risks and real possibilities. I found mine while inside a mass of earthbound snow, on an ice climb near Banff. While the general snow pack stability was moderate, meaning an avalanche was "not likely", it had snowed several inches the evening before. I struck out with a sixth sense that something might happen, and so I was particularly cautious. Despite the hazard, something was calling me forward. Just below the top of the route, three hundred meters from the ground and at the base of a large funnel of avalanche slopes, my wife yelled, "avalanche!" – an exclamation I had always dreaded. I had just anchored to the ice when a seemingly endless tube of powder snow enveloped us, sucking the air out of my gasping lungs. Initially, I was amazed that the torrent had not torn us from the ice. I then found myself free of panic and fear, with the surprising thought "not today, I have a contribution to make to the people who need me." At that moment I knew why I had come to the ice that day, why I was alive and what my future would promise.

I am building my business around the faithful notion that "entrepreneurs have a contribution to make to clients that need them." *In any enterprise, we must rise out of blind faith through crises of faith, on our way to building a conscious faith and confidence in ourselves and others.*

Optimizing the Law of Diminishing Returns

When I was a product designer, I spent two months in a plastic factory in Canton, Ohio, preparing for the production of a computer-controlled baby bassinet. During this time, I got to know the quality-control manager pretty well. One day he showed me some plastic molded parts that one of his other clients – the Toyota Motor Company – had rejected. He defied me to find the flaws in the parts, and surely I could not until he pointed them out underneath a microscope. Wow, I thought. What does this sort of pickiness really contribute to the customer experience, to real quality?

We live in the age where companies like Motorola are still striving to create what they call six-sigma quality – even in their cafeteria. The sigma is a statistical measurement of error: the sixth standard deviation of a normal curve: one error in many millions of trials or 99.999% right.

The "cult of perfection" drives the need to get things right the first time. This seems to be more efficient since things never have to be repeated. Presumably, perfect decisions require perfect information, which does not exist (well, it might at Motorola and Toyota, but it does seem to at my company). For human beings, what this does is cause all kinds of unneeded stress. It also delays action because people get caught up in researching and analyzing information, for fear of being wrong and for need of saving face.

The law of diminishing returns means that it takes roughly the same effort to move from complete ignorance to mostly right as it does to move from mostly right to absolutely right. At some point it is easier to correct an error than it is to try to avoid making it. Sometimes it is better to avoid doing anything at all. Peter Drucker, who arguably created the discipline of business management, said once that there is nothing more useless than perfecting something that does not need to be done in the first place.

The problem, of course, with using perfect information to make decisions is the inherent inaccuracy of the data. Information is often the result of events that have occurred in the past. Most of the interesting decisions in a venture relate to the future and how to make it kinder to us. We just do not have that kind of information.

A more interesting kind of decision is the entrepreneurial decision. Such a decision is far from perfect because we make it on the basis of sufficiency. The entrepreneurial decision is 80% confident. *In the context of a quickly unfolding, ambiguous future, a good decision is one that gets made and one where the results of error are recoverable.* Such decisions are smaller, graduated decisions that are iterative. It takes as much effort to make five 80% confident decisions as one 99% confident decision. Thus we get further in the venture by making many decisions that are good enough.

In this kind of process, we approach the future with an experimental attitude. Nothing replaces the value of the experiment: the prototype and the pilot test with live prospects. We cannot hypothesize our way into the future. Life itself is a series of trials. Like Edison and the countless trials leading to the invention of the light bulb, what we can do is always be prepared to recover from our supposed failures. This means that doing many smaller trials is more important and efficient than one larger trial that expends all our resources. The role of research is to assure a good experiment design, rather than to replace the experiment with obsessive analysis.

An experimental approach places a premium on wisdom and judgment over the analysis of constantly changing information. An entrepreneurial decision is a good decision. And if it is wrong, we can recover and make another one.

Overcoming the Rush to Market

The past five years have seen the arrival of the Internet time style, a compressed time scale that set a fire of panic amongst entrepreneurs terrified of losing a market window of opportunity. The fear that someone else will beat them to market causes many teams to cut corners during development, ignoring prudent research, testing and refinement on their path to an accelerated launch. First mover advantage has proven to be a fallacy in many market spaces. Either the pioneer rushes in and makes all kinds of errors that the second mover learns from as they step over the carcass, or the market space is large enough for a number of players.

This panicked approach to rushing a product to market is hardly new. Back in the late '80s, a company in Western Canada was attempting to get into the business of equipping buses with video entertainment systems. Their product consisted of VCRs, aisle-slung television monitors and headphone stations on the back of every seat. The company successfully raised venture capital through a public offering and developed their first prototypes. They installed one on their own bus as a demo system, so that customers could experience the system firsthand.

The company worked hard for months to develop the system and to arrange the first demonstration of the system. The president and vice-president of one of the largest bus carriers agreed to fly into town to try out the system. For days before the event, the quickly constructed prototype was up and running well. Everyone hoped the demo would be a great success and would lead to a sizable trial order that would launch their business and send their stock soaring. The day arrived. The system gleamed. Months of development work and investment were hanging on the demo. Important decision makers in suits arrived. They got on the bus, saw the gleaming system, sat down and were ready to be impressed. The driver started the bus, turned on the system and drove away. Each of the Suits put their headphones on. The movie, the sound, the entertainment impressed them. Then the bus hit a pothole in the road, causing the wireless seat-back receivers to go from picking up the movie sound track to picking up a country and western radio station. With some scrambling, the sales people managed to save the presentation and made a deal-in-principle. When the bus returned, the Suits filed off the bus. But as the last man, a tall man, their president, was leaving, he bashed his head open on a television hanging in the aisle of the bus and then canceled the order in the gore of the moment.

Months later, a well-padded television hung in the bus. They somehow managed to get a second chance with the Suits. This time, days before the demo, the system was crashing frequently and without warning, but there was no backing out. Rescheduling would erase any credibility remaining. Technicians worked around the clock to get the system working. Miraculously, minutes before the first people walked on the bus, the system started working. They toured the city, and just as the last person left the bus, the system crashed. Together, they wrote up a sizable deal, and the company drove its stock up and made dozens of paper millionaires. In the end, they did not appreciate their luck. Many poorly-handled business details sunk the company and the lead it had over its competitors. They never recovered. A handful of second-wave companies came in, corrected the errors and thrived.

In the end, there is often plenty of room in a market space for a number of strong competitors. *While it seldom works to be last-to-market, it is more lucrative to be the best-to-market than to be the first-to-market and the first-to-fail.*

Most of us in business have participated at one time or another
in the time-honoured tradition of listening to a motivational
speaker. Anthony Robbins thrusting his fist in the air and
yelling something about "giving it 110%" comes to my mind.
The problem with such high-intensity events is they are like
sugar highs that often leave us with less energy than we
started with. Like the proverbial Chinese food meal, we are
hungry again in an hour.

Motivational events have as their purpose the idea of
getting us moving more rapidly towards our goals. Sometimes it
is just about setting goals. Most speakers in the success industry
have pointed out that the bulk of people do not have clear
goals or a vision. Whether vision is clear or not, I am sure that
many people have desires that go unrequited. Anyone who has
made New Year's resolutions is most likely aware of the
feeling of failing to fulfill them. At that time of year, many
people set up a large number of hopes and expectations for the
future that erode into episodes of self-hate and resentment. It
seems that most of the goals have to do with health, losing
weight or otherwise conforming to society's expectations of us:
gotta do more, gotta be more.

As entrepreneurs, if we write plans, we specify the
vision for the future. This vision often has sales and growth
targets and paints, hopefully, a clear picture of where we
would like to be three to five years in the future. For those who
do not have a written, explicit plan, the vision often exists as
an image in the mind. In both cases, the vision is intended to
guide action towards the desired ends.

The difficulty lies in being really clear about what we
want and what we have in us to create. Without such clarity,
it is easy to lapse into the pursuit of default goals: what
parents, friends, or society as a whole tell us we should be and

what we should want. These exogenic drivers – goals that arise from outside influences – are not sustainable. As we move to achieve them and encounter the inevitable challenges, fears, doubts and setbacks, we find that we do not have the motivation to move forward. We hit the wall and that is how many of us end up in seminars, looking for the illusive truth and the magic path to happiness and success.

The motivational speakers are starting to lose appeal because external motivation is often just a short-term adrenaline boost. It is not a panacea, and there are no quick fixes.

What does work is a long-term commitment to creating real value. This means becoming clear on what we really want, what is most important to us and what we stand for. These are endogenic drivers – core values that come from within us. For example, if someone has a core value of family or balance, then they are internally motivated to create these. Trying to motivate this person to do anything in violation of their values, such as working long hours, will not work for long. At some point cajoling, cash bonuses and other lures become uninteresting. They run counter to the individual's internal drives. Reorganizing work, granting appropriate rewards and setting authentic goals that enhance rather than erode that person's values of family and balance will be motivating, not because someone is outside yelling "rah! rah!" but because vision and values are consistent. The person is then free to focus their natural life force towards the achievement of a purpose worthy of them and not one originating from someone else.

When we create a vision in alignment with our true personal values and not with social defaults, we find that we have ample motivation to navigate any problems on our path to fulfillment. My values work because they are mine. I appreciate all the coaching and support and I can get to help me reach my goals, but I do not rely on external motivation; I already have ample drive within.

Building Feasible Products in Real Time

Among my favourite product flops are "Spravy" aerosol gravy and "Toaster Eggs." What fascinates me is that each of these strange products was at sometime the passionate pursuit of some inventor or product manager genuinely believing they were on a path to change the world. I myself, for some much needed cashflow at the start of my design career, took on the project of building watches for dogs and I have been apologizing for that ever since. A few products it seems are easy to forecast, at least in retrospect. Generally, it is difficult to gauge in any market what magical mixtures of product and service features will woo an audience and which ones will lead to bankruptcy. In the time it takes to build a new service in response to a change in technology, competitive environment or customer demand, the very same forces prompting the changes may have changed themselves.

A feasibility study reviews the fit of a new business concept within the context of its changing environment. A good assessment does not address the question "if" a concept is viable but "how" it could be on five fronts: how we attract customers, how we make agreement, how we organize to deliver, how we satisfy users and how we profit. Having met many creative people, developers and inventors, I can report that the enemy of such vital review is often either a fear of judgment or an arrogance in thinking they have a more astute sense of customer tastes than customers themselves.

Many new programs fail for very simple reasons, because they lacked the cold eyes of an external review prior to a large investment into their launch. I once worked on a motorized baby bassinet that genuinely helped colicky babies sleep. The inventor had first licensed his idea to an American company. They invested millions to manufacture the first run of units only to find out that the US Consumer Product Safety

Commission would not approve the choice to run high-voltage into the product. It seems that a life-threatening shock and fire hazard does not go well with newly borne babies and is not a good marketing angle. The solution to this problem turned out to be simple and easy for us to find and took only some research and a few generations of prototypes.

Good product and service development is parallel process of studying feasibility and building prototypes. A prototype, whether for a physical product or a service, allows us to learn how to make something work without going to the large expense and taking the risk of going into production to see. Prototyping is iterative, that is, when we build a prototype, we are not doing so just to see if it works. We are doing so to understand its underlying principles – how it can work. The first one we build, or the first idea we try might not work. The point is to learn something so we can try again and again, until we crack the code and dial in a final design: research, build, test, learn, repeat.

The key element in this process is the time required to complete and repeat the cycle. Instead of just launching a new service into a new market space – a very expensive single trial that could break the program and lead us out of business – we can break down the research and development process into a larger series of smaller steps, cycles or iterations, learning many smaller lessons that ultimately lead to a favourable, less risky and ironically faster launch. In a service business a prototype represents a new way to deliver value to a client. We can describe the service idea in a Power Point presentation, as a colourful story or scenario, as a script describing the steps in the service, as a flowchart, spreadsheet or full-on experimental trial with a visionary client. *What we learn from rapidly building and testing new service prototypes in real time are the secrets to making the proposed venture more attractive, agreeable, deliverable, satisfying and profitable.*

Many service providers are very strong in the backend of their businesses, relating to the creation and delivery of their services.   Indeed, many practitioners become practitioners precisely because they enjoy the work with clients and resist or resent the marketing and selling front-end of their businesses. Most rely heavily on incoming referrals and are at the mercy and whim of their client bases.   A smaller client base, below critical mass, may not generate enough referrals.   A mature client base, that generates enough work, may not generate referrals that fit the definition of an ideal client and project. Referrals, almost by their nature, are passive and reactive and are largely beyond our control.   It is easy to lapse into a stagnant path, with the same old services and the same old clients.

Any proactive business actively seeks to penetrate new market segments with new product offerings. This is a practical necessity because clients, technology and the competitive environment are constantly in flux.   What works today for a certain kind of client will in time cease to be interesting or satisfying.   The approach to breaking into new areas depends on whether the market is a frontier or mature and on whether the product is tangible or intangible, personal or commercial.

The first dimension relates to the novelty of the segment itself.   In a frontier market, customers are largely unaware of their need for something.   They might have identified a problem, but they have not articulated what the problem is.   The coaching industry, for example, is still a frontier market, although it is maturing to where people are acknowledging that their stress in personal or business life ought to be prompting a change.   In time and for many, this need to change will evolve into a clear need to hire a professional coach. Just as entrepreneurs would see a tax or financial item as an issue for their accountant or financial planner and a contract as an issue for their lawyer, they will come to see stress and the fulfillment of new visions as issues for their coach. In frontier markets, the focus of marketing and sales tends to be on educating prospects so they come to appreciate both the nature of their particular needs and the appropriateness of the product as their solution. A mature market, where the needs are more obvious, tends to attract greater competition, and the emphasis changes from eduction to competitive differentiation among vendors.

The second dimension relates to the intangibility of the product offer. Purchasing a car is obviously tangible. People can directly sense the benefits of ownership. A pure service like coaching requires more imagination on the part of the buyer to perceive value. Marketing a service requires more emphasis on the core values of the company and less emphasis on the features of the service. Samples of the service help a prospect experience benefits before purchasing, not unlike a test drive.

The third dimension relates to the degree of personal involvement people have with the product. Commercial products are often a practical, bottom-line, results-oriented purchase. Most consumer products are more personal and feature a degree of passion. This sways the purchasing behaviour from a primarily logical process to a primarily emotional process, where logic is only used post-purchase to justify the expenditure. Personal products require a respectful and subtle approach to deal with sometimes vulnerable emotions, whereas commercial products can exploit a more direct and practical approach. For example, it can be more difficult to sell personal coaching than it is to sell business coaching because of the emotions involved in personal issues.

Breaking new ground with highly personal and intangible services in a frontier market is probably the most challenging and thus least crowded opportunity to create new business and ease reliance on referrals.

Dialing In the System

During the final years of my industrial design education, it became obvious to me that there were few if any jobs in the local market. Industrial design is the design of the things of industry and so naturally benefits from the presence of industry. Southern Alberta in the late '80s, despite all of the rhetoric about diversifying the oil and gas economy, was largely bereft of any major manufacturing presence. Most of the interesting industry came from startups, helmed by maverick entrepreneurs seeking to break into some global market.

I launched my own consulting business, while still in school, when a number of these pioneers contacted me looking for assistance. As both a novice designer and novice entrepreneur I proceeded with blind enthusiasm in learning whatever it took to become successful. It took me roughly eight years, six dozen projects, a stable of patient clients, a smaller number of pissed-off ones, three separate failed companies and a bankruptcy to make every single possible error there was. By 1996, we mastered our business and our design group sat atop its market with high sales, premium rates, credibility, cash in the bank and international awards.

Business is like a golf swing. It feels good to hit the ball well, but there are so many small parts to go wrong. A good golf swing is the "simple" matter of doing about sixty small things well, all at the same time. My partners and I used to joke that a successful project was just the absence of mistakes, where we did not do "this" wrong or "that" wrong, each of those things being a major business lesson. These lessons were hard to learn, like the lesson about getting really busy with projects and forgetting to sell, or not understanding bookkeeping, financial control and the seemingly subtle difference between cashflow and profit (as in not having the cash to pay taxes). I remember laughing off a mentor's suggestion that one day I would put my payroll on my Visa, until it happened. I fell into every hole in the road, and being young and resilient, I bounced out of them quickly. Translating a concept into an economically-feasible business in an unpredictable enterprise.

The Avante humidifier is a product I worked on, which is now in thousands of homes and has distribution across North America. The idea began as a patent for a new kind of humidifying mechanism and seemed quite simple, intuitive and elegant. The problem was it did not work. At the time of its invention, most home humidifiers had foam pads that would clog up with a miserable, smelly mess of gunk and were difficult and annoying to change.

The Avante invention was to feature a water wheel with a number of scoops. The wheel would dip into the water, each scoop would fill up with water and as it dumped its contents at the top, air would flow through the ensuing cascade and carry the fresh vapor through into the home. Sounded great to us, but we still insisted on testing it, and found out, with some dismay, that the device only evaporated the water in the bottom of the tray; the wheel and scoops were redundant. This finding was of no comfort to the company which was in the process of going public.

We worked as a team for months, trying experiment after experiment until the science of a new type of wheel emerged. This design featured a parallel array of serrated discs that, as they dipped into the water, picked up a thin film of water which would then evaporate. This new invention worked well, earning international distribution and its own new patents, to which my father likes to say his son has a patent on the wheel. *An innovation is often the result of many iterations of dedicated art and science getting closer and closer to some new working idea and important breakthrough.*

Surviving the Entrepreneurial Moment

The book *Touching the Void* by the alpine climber Joe Simpson is one of the best mountain survival stories ever written. He and his partner were pioneering a new route in a very remote area of South America, supported only by a base camp cook and a donkey, which had brought them the many miles they had traveled from any semblance of civilization.

They got to the summit many days after their planned food ran out. Weary after days of numbing cold and uncertain survival, Joe slipped over an ice cliff during the descent and smashed his leg. His partner, Simon, lowered him down the descent route during a blinding storm by settling into the snow and paying the rope out around his waist, as Joe hung on the tense line, slowly inching his way down to the glacier below.

At one point in the descent, Simon inadvertently lowered Joe over a cliff. With Joe hanging in mid air, the sudden increase in load was slowly pulling Simon out of his stance. Such an event would lead to certain death for both of them, so Simon made the very difficult choice of cutting the rope, setting Joe into a freefall for several hundred feet. Distraught and on the edge of his own survival, Simon searched fruitlessly for Joe, and then finally left for base camp and the long journey back to civilization. What Simon did not know is that Joe had actually fallen into a deep crevasse and landed on a soft snow bridge which had miraculously broken his fall. The rest of the story is about Joe's will to live despite the almost certain knowledge that Simon had left base camp thinking that his partner had perished.

I have touched the same void during isolated and fortunately short-lived moments as an ice climber. On one particular outing, I was planning to climb a short but nasty pillar of ice that was known to turn back even the best of local ice climbers. As I approached the dagger of ice, hanging free from a lip of ancient limestone, I spotted an ice screw that had been abandoned for some reason by a previous party. Since I was in university and poor at the time, I welcomed any opportunity to find expensive climbing gear. As I got nearer the pillar I learned why the screw was there, as the ice below it was streaked in some unfortunate climber's blood, portending a similar fate for me if I was anything other than immaculately focused and competent. Being young, I ignored the obvious warning and started up the climb anyway.

This was one of the nastiest climbs I ever led. Every movement and placement of my ice tools had so little margin for error that the route demanded every fiber of concentration and physical strength I could muster. After what seemed like a fairly short elapse of time, I climbed to a safe set of bolts drilled into the rock at the top and relaxed for the first time. I did not recall having even one errant thought; I had my mind sharply focused on upward progress and avoiding a plummet to the ground seventy five feet below my feet. My belayer later informed me that I had been climbing for two and a half hours.

Like most entrepreneurs I have been in some tight spots as an entrepreneur: how to save a failing product, untie a severe cash-flow knot or deal with a hostile client. At the time these crises feel as impossible and life threatening as the day I spent climbing above someone's bloodstained error. Freezing my view on the ground below would not have worked and would only have assured that fate. *Forward progress through a seemingly impossible crisis does not result from the distraction of obsessing on failure but from a focus on and faith in some unforeseen path to safety and success.*

Getting into the Flow of Conscious Living

Death scares the crap out of me sometimes. In moments of terror it seems like a big black hole sucking me into a hopeless oblivion. The first time I felt this way was the first time I went into a cemetery as a teen. I would not let myself look at the headstones, as if the finality of someone else's resting place would somehow trap me into the same fate. I remember the same feeling as a young adult, viewing the lifeless body of Bill March, the leader of Canada's first Everest Expedition, who had fallen not from a high mountain but from a brain aneurysm on the flat trail out from one. Bill had been so alive when I last saw him. Then, I had the impression that his essential "Billness" had left his body and gone somewhere. I did not know where it went, but I hoped it is somewhere good.

On my thirty-fifth birthday, I began a process to accept my own fateful death. This acceptance is not intellectual, it is the felt experience, however vague, of my continuity in some form, of my being in some kind of flow. Demographically, I think this spiritual awakening happens somewhere in an entrepreneur's mid-thirties. At that time, the fortieth birthday looms not so distantly and it is but a short hop into the big sleep. It got me thinking about my spiritual views and almost forced me to ponder the great questions of why I am here and what it all means.

Prior to this realization, as an immortal teenager and young adult, I had effectively cordoned off this whole line of thinking, so I could focus on what teenagers and young adults tend to focus on. But I do remember a particularly astute high school English teacher who read us a poem about death. A man was riding alone on a horse down the path of his elder years. He looked into the darkness of the forest, adjacent to his path. In the dim light of the forest he saw his death. He did not flee, as he might have as a younger man, but saw death's friendly welcome – the reward for a life lived well. In time, death comes to us all. As we have lived, so shall we come to embrace it in the end.

Recently I had occasion to wander through a cemetery. Something had changed. I saw burial plots of single people gone, years past. I saw couples buried together; sometimes the end dates were close, sometimes the survivor had lived on for years. And in other pairings, a partner had gone, but was patiently waiting to reunite with its living mate, with only the remnant's birthday carved into the granite – the blank space to its right seeming to call out for some final act. In time, the pairing would be complete, and the masons would get their chance to scribe the final date in its proper place. I then imagined someone, some years later, viewing my own place next to my wife, wondering who these people were and what they did and what kind of influence they had on those around them and on the world at large. I understood my purpose in life was to live well and in such a way that the people left behind by my passing would find it in themselves to come and pay homage and tribute.

The only viable solution to the dread of death is to choose to live well. *It is only through conscious living that we come to appreciate the value of life, its passing and our continuity in some eternal flow – the feeling of timeless, spaceless bliss.* Flow is our chance to transcend the spatial and temporal limits of the purely material life, to sample what might lie beyond and move through the black hole into the zone of creation. Whatever we create and achieve are the spawn of this black hole of death, as they seem to flow out of from the same void into which we ourselves are flowing. Everything comes from nothing and nothing comes from everything. Unresolved feelings towards death only undermine the passion of creative flow. It is the acceptance of the pending demise of life and its creations that predicates their value to us; we appreciate what will be lost.

Several years ago, my wife and I decided to try ski mountaineering. As competent skiers yet new to the glacial ski environment, we chose to go up with a mountain guide, my longtime friend Karl Nagy. With Karl's help, we chose a peak in the Roger's pass that was both beautiful and challenging. We sat in the valley the day before and plotted a route through to the summit.

At dawn we strapped on special skis and avalanche beacons that Karl had brought for us. Before we left we practiced finding a decoy avalanche beacon, pretending to be buried skiers. Then we embarked on our journey.

It was during the ascent that I came to appreciate the true value of our guide. I am always impressed by how different a mountain looks up close, how easy it is to lose the route and how dangerous a misstep can be. From afar, the route looked straightforward to the summit. On that morning, we navigated a twisted system of ridges, slopes, gullies and glaciers standing in the way of the big view. Karl always found the best way through the maze, one that minimized the strain on our calves as we pierced upward and avoided the many dangers en-route. A glacier poses the hazard of falling into crevasses – the deep, wedged-shaped cracks deviously waiting to swallow unsuspecting tourists into an oblivion of cold sleep. These same steep, snow-laden slopes, wait for the same sloppy tourists to trigger the pent-up forces of tons of white death. Depending on the time of day, the wind, the temperature, the preceding week's weather, its time in the sun, its angle relative to the sun's rays, any given slope can be safe or not. One might be bombproof in the morning and a death trap in the afternoon. Another might be safe on the right side and a burial plot on the left. Karl knew the difference between safe and dangerous, even when the margin was slim.

We did not need anyone to drag us up the mountain, to tell us which peak we found inspiring or to teach us how to ski (although his encouragement and tips were welcome). We needed someone on the other end of the rope, watching out for us. With Karl, we skied and climbed mountains we might not have otherwise attempted because we lacked his gift of route finding, his experience of risk management and the tools and tricks of his trade. He was solid, he was safe and he always brought us home more alive. He followed our lead and then we followed his.

In the end, both climbing and commerce are inherently risky ventures. In business, not every good idea works and not every new project ends in success. In the mountains, it is not just a matter of avoiding danger. To do that, we could have simply stayed in the hot tub, going nowhere and dying excruciatingly slow, monotonous deaths. To really live is to risk danger and sometimes even death. And sometimes death calls the great ones. In a perverse twist of fate, Karl died in a freak accident.

Karl's memory continues to inspire my own work to accompany entrepreneurs to the summits of their own ventures, in the mountains of entrepreneurial pursuits. It has been challenging for me to contribute leadership to people pioneering great innovations in their fields of endeavour. As a younger person, new to the coaching business, my well-meaning attempts to invent and push visions and values on people were tiring for me and irritating to the entrepreneurs already in possession of fine ones. As a more seasoned venture supporter, I aspire to provide a vehicle to assist people in finding safe and fast routes to entrepreneurial summits, otherwise too dangerous or difficult to climb alone. *Great guides, whether in the ventures of business or nature, remember where their people want to go, possess a sophisticated set of tools to get there and bring a hard-won experience in route finding, hazard evaluation and risk management.*

Many service providers cringe when they hear the words "selling" and "sales." These two words connote all sorts of dark images of plaid-coated hucksters, pawning all manner of unneeded and over priced-goods onto helpless prospects. "We are above selling" is the message implied by new age business cards sporting euphemisms such as "client care manager", "relationship specialist" or "director of client services." Businesses hide the agenda under these more palatable titles and then act surprised when people get suspicious and angry when the inevitable sales process rears its ugly head. Every business sells something to someone, and cloaking the sales process only erodes trust.

There is no question that the process of enrolling clients and making agreements had to change. Bad salesmen earned their sleazy reputations largely because they and their methods were pushy, officious and disrespectful. They belonged to an era when companies believed that they knew best what people wanted and pushed these products through to the end-consumer. We owe a debt of gratitude to millions of women who softened the hard sell by bringing respect and care into the process. Relationship selling sought to move the emphasis from the commercial transaction of commodity for money to the connection of human beings at a more personal and emotional level. This was a much needed shift towards greater respect. However the early models shunned the closing overtures, and the relationship never matured from personal rapport to commercial business.

All purchasing requires a moment of trust between vendor and customer. Service businesses, especially the innovative ones, face the stiffest sales challenge. First, it is often much easier to sell a tangible product. People can get their minds around something physical. Learning about an intangible service often requires imagination and patience and that requires more trust. Second, services tend to be more personal than many tangible or commercial products. Any product that is personal requires more emotional vulnerability than an impersonal commercial product and that also requires more trust. Third, services are often in service of latent needs, targeted at the sophisticated motives lying just under the surface of the prospect's consciousness and that certainly requires more trust.

People commit only to the degree that they trust in the vendor. While people have a default level of trust in other people, trust does grow with time. The real value in relationship selling is the scaling of trust and thus the forging of commitment over time: starting with small commitments and eventually letting trust blossom. Each step in the relationship building process is a unique client contact moment, a distinct verse in a larger conversation heading toward eventual commitment of time, energy and money in the relationship. This process can be done quickly, but only if we do not skip steps: it is often easier and faster to take many small steps than a few large ones. We reduce friction, blocks and gaps in the process – any point that a prospect is tempted to exit the sales conversation – by including more steps that make it easier to climb. If there is a point in the process where people are not moving through, it means there was not enough trust for the prospect to justify taking the next step. Every step is risky and requires a commitment. Asking for something too big, too early in the process can lead to the prospect abandoning the process.

Every step in the process requires a clear and safe action. This means breaking the process of buying and selling – finding a way to be of service to someone – into a series of smaller commitments, each with a smaller but clearer intention. *A smooth sales process is a graduating process of many small steps, each with the intention of increasing trust and commitment towards a mutually beneficial commercial relationship.*

Balancing Good Leadership and Good Management

Venture capitalists, angel investors and other people interested in and affected by entrepreneurs will tell you that the people who identify new ideas, marshal resources to pursue them and establish the initial thrust into the unknown are rarely the people who will execute them profitably. Likewise, the professional managers who maintain stable, thriving businesses are rarely the people who identify the opportunities to change the venture into something more valuable. Hence exists the difference between leaders and managers and the tenuous balance that must be struck between them. The difference between good management and good leadership and the key to their balance may be held in a continuum of two distinct yet compatible views of creativity: between chaos and order.

A leader might define creativity as anything that is original. This is the more glamorous and traditional view of creation: something is not creative unless it is new, different and plucked from the ether of the mysterious unknown. Leaders under this definition follow murky paths into the frontiers of knowledge and commerce. Good leaders disturb the continuity of the status quo to bring about a higher level of future continuity. Leading charge into new, unchartered territory, they are driven to pioneer the new products, markets and processes arising from a changing world. To lead, from this perspective, is to craft a vision of some new opportunity for productive change and higher value.

This drive towards greater complexity energizes the enterprise for change. Change is exciting to pioneers, who are prone to boredom and to either prematurely moving on to the next new thing or shaking up the existing thing before it has a chance to deliver on the promise of its new value. They resist the structure required to make the new idea consistent, reliable and stable. Maverick entrepreneurs, avoiding the cramped and mundane feeling of infrastructure, will often lose motivation just before they have returned on the investments of people who had followed them into the void. Some chaos leads to productive change. Too much chaos makes an innovation too complex and scary to finish.

Conversely, a manager might define creativity as anything that is operable. From this perspective, only the practical and simple ideas that become something real and tangible are worthy. Managers, under this definition, complete the innovation by helping customers and staff accept the value proposition and make it part of their lives. It is not enough to be new, the business has to deliver. The drive towards greater order brings the venture to a steady-state of consistent profits. But structure, the keep of the professional manager, is also often the very enemy of new innovation. Managers make huge investments of time, energy and money into infrastructure. This investment gives a certain inertial quality to the structure that is a barrier to any change to it. Managerial protection yields the required profit in the short-term but also prevents change and improvement that is also required in the long-term. Some order leads to stability and consistent cash-flow. Too much order dissipates the energy and excitement required for the periodic restructuring demanded by a business environment that is in constant flux.

Without both inspired leadership and solid management a venture would not respond well to nor profit from changes in its environment. Powerful leadership identifies exciting opportunities from the chaos of constantly changing customers, technology, competitors. Powerful management brings about the eventual innovation from the order of simple stable infrastructure. *A business endures, past its startup and again through the transitions dictated by a rapidly changing business environment, by striking a balance between the chaos of good leadership and the order of good management.*

Working a Model for Volitional Mechanics

In his book *Good to Great,* Jim Collins develops the metaphor of a flywheel to describe what is feels like to be inside a company making a transition through time to the highest levels of performance. A flywheel is a large, heavy disk that spins horizontally on an axis and has great inertia. To move the wheel from its resting state takes tremendous effort, but once the wheel is turning, it is easier to turn and gathers momentum until it is very difficult to stop. If it is spiraling in one direction, regardless of whether that is negative or positive, it wants to stay moving in that direction.

People and organizations likewise have inertia and at any time are moving in upward or downward spirals. Most of us periodically have the experience of being "caught in a loop", a stressful experience that feels like a flywheel turning against us. It takes tremendous effort to slow down, halt and reverse the spin of the wheel and create the equivalent of an upward spiral. There are some forces that are working against us and drive the wheel in a negative direction and there are some working for us and seeking to spin the wheel positively. Each force is a vector, with a certain magnitude and direction. Engineers call this "field force analysis", the study of all the forces acting on a body, ultimately determining direction. If the positive forces are stronger than the negative forces the outcome will be positive. A positive outcome adds more rotational momentum to the wheel and it take less force to maintain or even increase the speed of the wheel. When our flywheels are spinning quickly in the positive direction, we are in the flow of positive experiences and positive results and more invulnerable to the setbacks that might otherwise send us into a negative spin.

The "flywheel affect" illustrates relational dynamics, especially during the sales process between client and service provider. Imagine a sales situation where I am proposing a workable solution to a client who has a problem and the resources to solve it. In this situation, I either make a deal or I do not and then I solve the problem or I do not. The results "make a deal and solve the problem", "make a deal and fail to solve the problem" and "fail to make a deal" are the possible outcomes.

Outcomes reflect the combined intentions of the people involved. Deepak Chopra, in describing the system of karma and dharma, and, Gary Zukav, in describing the spiritual implications of quantum physics, both arrive at the same conclusion: intentions determine results. Results betray the net effect of all intentions whether positive or negative, conscious or unconscious.

Shared thoughts, attitudes and beliefs drive outcomes. Some beliefs support the results we say we want and some do not. Beliefs convey intentions. For example, the two beliefs "this will never work" and "there is always a way" form a dialectic, as do the thoughts "there is not enough to go around" and "there is enough for everyone." If I were to approach a sales situation with the two negative beliefs, I would quite certainly prove them out: it would indeed not work and there would not be enough to go around. I would fail and then subsequently starve and the client would still have a problem. The flywheel would spin around negatively and make it more likely that I approach the next situation with the same negative thinking. If the client has the same doubt, we secure a negative result. If we vacillate between the positive and negative thinking, the outcome will reflect the sum of our vectors. If I take the other more positive positions, and my intentions are aligned with the best intentions of the other person, they will play themselves out as positive spins on the wheel: it will work and there will be abundance for everyone. *Every result, whether positive or negative, is the net effect of all negative and positive intentions, beliefs and attitudes that accumulate and build momentum through time.*

Dan Millman, in his book *No Ordinary Moments,* offered a non-pathological definition of addiction. Severe clinical addictions such as alcoholism, drugs and gambling have complex psychological, physiological and sociological factors and are the appropriate target of therapists, twelve-step programs and other social programs. These programs see acute addiction as a disease that must be remedied. Millman's thoughts are hopeful and positive: an addiction is any behaviour we use to dissipate the creative energy that we are not using for creative purposes. Many addictive behaviours are a natural and normal part of being human. Every person who is creative has some addictions.

Creative energy, the energy of passion and of being alive, flows through all of us. Its purpose is to find a constructive outlet. Such outlets of course exist everywhere: the traditional arts, the professions, the trades and in friendly and family relationships. In all of these fields it is possible to create something positive, to make an affirmative contribution to the people around us, to the collective culture, to society as a whole and even to the greater planet. There is no shortage of opportunities to contribute and create, but we seldom do so constantly and consistently. It is simply not possible and may not even be desirable to be always on the positive side of life. Bad days punctuate good ones. These are the cycles of life. What is desirable is learning to consciously reengage in our own creative process.

During those moments when we are not fully engaged in constructive behaviours that make an affirmative contribution, our creative energy has no outlet. It begins to build up in our bodies creating a bloated, constipated feeling. Writer's block is probably the most famous illustration of blocked creativity, with writers being some of the most infamous addicts. Since the human body does not store energy well, we get to the point where the pent up energy has to complete a circuit. So instead of coming out of the "front door" and applying its force on a worthwhile external project, it comes out of a "back door exit " in the form of habitual practices, designed to burn off or leak out the excess energy. This creative energy takes the form of overwork, overexercise, overspending and gambling (and then having to overwork to pay of the bills), overeating, sex, drugs and alcohol. While all of these behaviours can destroy relationships and ultimately the person using them, they all can start out as misapplied creativity expressing energy through metabolic and physical action.

I can use my energy for creative or destructive ends. An addiction is a limiting behaviour that becomes compelling and compulsive over time. A clinical addiction grows in the darkness of shame that results from choosing the addictive behaviour over a creative one. When I choose to disengage from a creative outlet, at some level, I offend the value system I possess that demands creative expression. Since taking full ownership of my opportunities is sometimes a daunting act of self-respect and intimacy, I do not always choose the high road. I risk plummeting into an accelerating downward spiral of self-hate and gradual destruction. The spiral may be slow and unobtrusive at first, but with continued indifference to the opportunities to create value, I escalate the downward spiral. At some critical point it becomes easier to repeat the behaviour and "get the hit" than find the will to reengage in meaningful activity. What was once an ineffective habit, limiting self-expression and actualization, could, if left unsupported, becomes a clinical addiction requiring the intervention of professional therapists. *Prior to the onslaught of a prolonged creative draught and its resulting addictive behaviour, we all have the opportunity to reach out for the support we need to maintain and continually recommit to the full potential we have as creative beings.*

Overcoming Archaic Patterns of Self-Protection

When I was young, my friends and I tended to do everything in a big way. We once built a fort that was an elaborate construction with running water, electricity, a security system and an atrium. My mother named our collection of grandiose neighbourhood kids Cecil B. deMille, Big Productions – a reference to a movie producer who made huge epics but rarely completed a picture on budget or on time. I was not content to do anything the way everyone else did. My fort had to be different.

I take the position that each of us has a set of values core to our existence. These are the standards, principles and concepts that have pulled us through time with such urgency that they have become part of our characters. Compromising on a core value is a source of stress in my life, and taking a stand on it is the source and force of satisfaction. Distinction, justice, honesty, challenge or any core value can play out positively or negatively.

One of my core values is contribution – the commitment to making a bigger difference. As a writer, coach and speaker, I find making a bigger difference very satisfying. Making important contributions to the people around me is the source of my passion. I base my service on my ability to help companies differentiate themselves from their competitors by drawing out what is different and unique about them: the source of their passion and capacity to make a bigger difference. Other times, I just create or find a difference that makes no difference and no one cares about. This leads only to the experience of indifference. Passion and indifference are the two sides of the same value.

Carl Jung believed that each person has both a light and shadow side. In the light, people reflect affirmative beliefs and behaviours that support them in creating positive outcomes. The darker shadow side is the set of limiting beliefs and behaviours that undermine experience and cause negative results.

Unconscious limiting belief systems unwittingly generate self-destructive behaviours. Grandiosity is one of my main self-limitations and the shadow side of contribution, driven by the shadow belief that "nothing is ever good enough." "Never good enough" is like a program that runs through my mind, manifesting itself as visions and plans so big that they are impossible to complete. In the shadow of the incompletion I fail to make a bigger difference and then judge that I am not good enough. Each limiting belief reflects an insecurity and masks an archaic fear. I fear other people will corrupt my artistic creations. Any threat of mediocrity – where everything is the same – triggers this fear. To protect my ideas from being made common, I withhold them from people.

Overcoming fear requires strength. My strength – which is an ongoing struggle to develop – is in being grounded. Ironically, I only fear the corruption of ideas that are grandiose and impossible to fulfill anyway. When I am grounded, I have taken the position that "there is good, genius and beauty in everything." From this position, and connected to what is special and unique about someone, I am not insecure or afraid of corruption.

Until I make shifts at the belief level, my limiting patterns will persist. I may try to will my way into positive behaviours, but these will end the moment I trigger my fear. With practice and greater consciousness, I can change from thinking I am not good enough to thinking I am unique and special. I then differentiate myself, make a bigger difference and create passion rather than withdraw and create indifference. *When we overcome our limiting beliefs and connect to our more empowering beliefs, we behave in ways that add genuine value and make life and business easier, more fun and more lucrative.*

Switching into the Creative Space Between Comfort and Pain

In Greek mythology, the Muses were the nine daughters of Zeus and Mnemosyne who inspired music, poetry and drama. A Muse is the archetypal inspiration for any creative pursuit. To find one's muse is to tap into the sometimes evanescent creative source, from which all novelty and passion flow.

In his sweeping study of prominent creators and creations, the University of Chicago professor of psychology Mihaly Czikszentmihaly made striking connections between creative activity and the principles of his famous theory of flow. Flow is the state of optimal experience marked by a feeling of timelessness, intense focus and deep joy: a state we all enter as we match our skills to an appropriate challenge. Flow is a narrow sliver that exists between the less optimal states of boredom and anxiety. Boredom comes from a well-developed skill set misapplied to a weak challenge, and anxiety comes from a skill set that is not up to an overwhelmingly difficult challenge.

Two requirements of flow are clear autotelic goals – goals that emanate from within – and a measurement mechanism that provides clear, unambiguous feedback regarding immediate success and failure. In the creative realm of business, an autotelic vision is borne of the core values shared by the entrepreneurs and their customers. The measurement of success comes from the judgments of clients, deciding whether to buy in or be satisfied once they do.

Inherent in the idea of flow is the notion of growth. Life is a game that is never quite won, an unrelenting and escalating field of practice and play. As we mature, our skills and competencies naturally increase as we apply more wisdom in their direction. This means that what once were fulfilling challenges become boring, and we must face steeper challenges to stretch us out of complacency. The stretch must be just large enough to place us back into a flow state without overwhelming our sense of confidence and placing us back into anxiety and perhaps even abject terror. This is the work of moving out of our comfort zones to create space for ever more challenging and rewarding endeavours. Such work is not a theoretical construct but a very pragmatic business of making commitments and taking action to move out of the zone of comfort into the space of optimal creativity.

Many people believe that they need to be under stress to gain the motivation to move forward. Indeed, leaving the completion of some important step until the last minute surely does light the proverbial fire, but the flow-perspective suggests that the experience of creation and the quality of the creative product will be far from optimal. In my way of thinking, all stress comes from the absence of a core value – from the absence of something we hold to be most important. In this sense, the stress is indeed the deeper motivator for creation, because it leads us to focus on what is most important to us, our autotelic goals. But we do not do an effective job of creating what is most important to us if we stay in our comfort zones, and neither do we create our best work if we are distressed by moving too rapidly out of it. Stress is just the guide to a place of higher value.

Creativity exists in the narrow zone between pain and comfort. A good mechanism to stretch the comfort zone without tearing it is to focus on activities that add new value to clients. On a scale of zero to ten, these action steps would be at a level of seven. Below this mark, the commitment is not bold enough to shake up complacency; above this level, the commitment would be so uncomfortable that we would risk not completing our task. *As we make commitments and set action steps that stretch our zones of comfort, we create the positive experience of moving forward and fulfilling the promise of our core values.*

Part IV: Contribution
Making a Bigger Difference

Creating Passion and Higher Margins

Focusing on Serving High Value Clients

When I was seven years old, I started my first venture. In the summer, on the street where I lived, every kid was out peddling lemonade and Kool-aid to all the other kids for 5¢ a glass. My best friend and I decided to enter the juvenile beverage business and corner the lemonade market. We raided our mothers' kitchens, set up our stand next to the series of others and proceeded to do what everyone else was doing. This was my introduction to a commodity marketplace: everyone selling the same product to the same people for the same price. Despite our mothers supplying all of the materials, no one was making any money. There were more vendors than customers and everyone was starving – though not thirsty, because we all drank our own product. Something had to change.

Our fortunes did change on one of those brutal, sweltering July days. I was fortunate to receive a major life lesson, the kind we tend to remember for a lifetime. I lived in a new neighborhood at the edge of a construction zone. Our stand was the last one in the "mall of lemonade stands" closest to the site. Every day we watched dump trucks drive in and out of the site. The drivers were big, burly, hot and sweaty. We did not think much of it until one day one of them stopped, inhaled a large glass of our finest, gave us 25¢ for the glass and then bought a second to quench the remainder of his thirst. We did not need to be told twice. My business partner and I moved our stand farther down the street to where the trucks slowed to make the turn. In no time, the word got out. We parlayed our first "beta" customer into a large base of customers. We had successfully penetrated the big, burly, hot and sweaty truck driver market, and we were selling lemonade to most of them. We had five times the number of clients buying five times the amount of product at five times the price. We were making so much money that we eventually diversified into selling doughnuts and chips, but we eventually just "ate" most of our profits.

This was my first lesson in business and target marketing: rather than operate in an overcrowded, low-margin market, we discovered a new high-value client base. As a market segment, big, burly, hot and sweaty truck drivers had a bigger "thirst" for our product (high-need) and had deeper pockets (high-money). We made a bigger difference to a bigger market and made bigger money as a result.

At some point in their careers, most entrepreneurs face the same dilemma – reconciling the twin drives of making a difference and making money. As we mature, and the sophistication of our ventures increase, we may find a deeper yearning to contribute. It seems we are blessed, or cursed, with both a need to "selfishly" profit from our creativity and "selflessly" contribute to others and even the planet. These are often at odds, but it is very possible to do well by doing good – to get paid really well doing what we are so passionate about we would have done it for free anyway. One way to do that is to serve clients with important and challenging problems that have ample capital to solve them. By serving these high-need, high-value clients, we make a big contribution solving the problem and we attract the high-money resources to create a high quality of life.

A criticism of this approach is that it is elitist and excludes the less fortunate from our best creative attention. I argue that if we are more tapped into the flow of abundance, we have the resources to assist others who are struggling to make their lives work It serves no one if we join the ranks of the impoverished. *By focusing on clients with the most stressful problems and the most resources to solve them, we build strong, healthy businesses that can spread the wealth to others who are less fortunate.*

The basic level and lower purpose of a business is the provision of some technical commodity. There is by definition not much inherently different or special about the commodity itself. The professional associations that govern accountants, lawyers, architects and other professionals exist to assure the consuming public that there is no qualitative difference between various professionals and that each perform their duties to a common set of standards. The association would deem the breech of any such standard as unethical and would take corrective action against the transgressor. Indeed, financial statements, legal proceedings and building plans ought to be held to high technical standards. Technical failures can lead to severe damage to the client.

Compliance to standards of conduct and competence, however, does not ensure a good experience. Technical prowess does not guarantee that the client's business shows a profit, or that the client receives a fair judgment or that the building is beautiful and fulfilling to inhabit. Such outcomes are the higher purpose of professionals like accountants, lawyers and architects. And these are not legislated by a professional association.

The relational level defines the higher purpose of the enterprise, the performance above and beyond technical competence. The commodity itself solves a technical problem, but at the relational level the business solves a personal problem. The standards that govern that kind of performance and good client and service provider relationships reflect the core values they share.

The coaching industry lacks formal standards of practice. Anyone can declare to the world that they are a coach. Droves of people are discovering this calling. While coaches have been supporting the performance of elite athletes for decades, personal and business coaches are emerging now to serve the needs of entrepreneurs, professionals, leaders and the general public. Our industry, like every new discipline capable of causing severe damage to people through technical incompetence, will eventually see a legislating body emerge to manage the ethics and morals of the profession and to oversee the process of deciding who becomes a so-called professional coach, what the educational requirements will be and how they must practice and intervene in the lives of their clients in a respectful manner. Until then, customers are on their own to make good purchasing decisions. The only differentiator will be the core values of the practitioner.

Anyone that chooses my services is attracted to the notion of contribution and what I call "making a bigger difference." Contribution is one of my precious concepts, something that I stand for and have felt tugging at me my whole life. This value drives me towards the experience of greater power and the result of higher momentum. I experience the absence of contribution as the feeling of overwhelm, of not moving forward and making the kind of impact I am capable of. My best clients have this same time-oriented stress. We have not leveraged the support and systems we have available to us and often get our high need for power met by being controlling. But because we all value contribution, we are naturally motivated to change and become a source of power to the people in our lives. The best way for me to experience power and make a bigger difference is to assist my customers in experiencing power and making a bigger difference.

Since I have spent my life in the pursuit of contribution, I have become adept at moving people forward in methodical step-by-step process that adds leverage, increases momentum and defeats feelings of overwhelm. *We create a satisfying experience for our customers by using our talents to alleviate stress.*

Turning Up the Value 78

Raising Prices

With one year left to complete my product design degree, and with no prospects for finding a job in my field, I decided to start my own product design consulting business. I had been working as a junior designer in another firm which had gone bankrupt, leaving several clients hanging. When they phoned me up looking for help, I was in business.

As an employee, I never had to deal with the often thorny issue of pricing. Now, as an entrepreneur I was faced with the challenge of setting my price and determining my value. I did my first few contracts at $40/hour, which I thought adequately reflected my experience and the fact I had not completed my degree. My price had nothing to do with the inherent value of the project or the results my clients needed, I based it on how confident and secure I felt, or, more accurately, how unconfident and insecure I felt. I was afraid to charge more and it showed.

There are three main ways to make more money: decrease costs, increase volume or raise prices. I quickly discovered that $40/hour was not enough to cover costs. To shore up my cash shortfalls, I took on more clients and contracts. Very soon after that, I was getting too busy and I began making costly errors. I was not making enough money to do a good enough job to even justify the low rates I was charging. The only solution was to raise prices.

I have come to appreciate, that at some level, people decide what they are worth. It can be difficult to rise above a self-appointed value limit. For most small service providers, the price issue can be especially sensitive. This is true because we are often providing the service ourselves. In effect, people are buying us. Increasing my price means that I think I am more valuable and is a challenge to any areas of low self-esteem I may be holding on to. We all have blocks to realizing our true

177

potential and value. Raising the bar on my price can draw out an anxious, doubtful feeling that "I am an impostor." Of course, it is those very attitudes, often unconscious, that undermine our value and limit our prices.

Sometimes the only way to raise prices is to simply do it, and then learn to live up to it. I may be uncomfortable with my new rate in the short term, but it sets a vision that I grow into: "How would someone worth this much behave?" Then I answer. In one sweeping move, I raised my rate from $40/hour to $90/hour. For several anxious months I wandered around waiting to be discovered as the fraud I felt I was. "Who am I to be worth this much money?" But in a very short time, something very interesting began happening. I began winning bids at these higher rates and my team and I found out afterwards that we were usually 40%-100% higher in price than our nearest competitor. What we had not noticed was that we had developed a very unique design approach, that our competitors did not have and that our clients believed was the best path to the results they sought. With a superior methodology and at these new price levels, we had fewer clients and enough time and money to do a really good job and create the expected results. The results we created were more valuable to our customers which, in their minds, justified the higher rates.

Price is the arbiter of supply and demand, controlling the flow of value between service provider and client. Clients deserve to pay more, because they deserve to receive greater value. Each of us has a set of core values that define what we think is most important. Values-based pricing frees us from the trap of commodity or market-based pricing and the insecurity of our self-worth. *If we choose clients that appreciate our core values and then design and operate our businesses based on these same values, we will naturally create more valuable results that warrant premium prices.*

Living a Complete Life

In a moment of black comedy, and what now seems to be a macabre prophecy, the comedian Denis Leary once said of his decision to move to New York City: "...there are so many ways to die in New York...it teaches you to live life the way it should be lived...moment to moment... ."

I cannot even get my mind around what it must be like to be inside a building as it plummets to the ground, or looking outside my window and watching as the plane I am in hurtles itself towards the very same building or being on the ground as huge chunks of that man-made structure fall to earth on the same path which I am running to flee. I do know that I would want my final thoughts to be with the people I am leaving behind, not on any unfinished business and certainly not on business.

September 11, 2001, will stand as a day that the world changed. And not all of the changes will be directed towards retributive violence, increased protectionism and xenophobia. While I join with most people around the world in condemning a diabolical and evil-spirited act of terrorism, I also think that many people will be ultimately shocked out of their complacency and may choose to live life more passionately and more engaged in the pursuit of what is most important to them.

Yvon Chouinard, the famed outdoorsman, entrepreneur and environmentalist, once wrote about industrial man's growing disconnection from himself and his world. "We are Homo Sapiens, the tool users. We earn the name by developing tools to increase our leverage on the world around us, and with this increased technological leverage comes a growing sense of power. This position of advantage which protects us from wild nature we call civilization. Our security increases as we apply more leverage, but along with it we notice a growing isolation from the earth. We crowd into cities which shut out the rhythms of the planet – daybreak, high tide, wispy cirrus high overhead yelling storm tomorrow, moonrise, Orion going south for the winter. Perceptions dull and we come to accept a blunting of feeling in the shadow of security. Drunk with power, I find that I am out of my senses. I, tool man, long for immediacy of contact to brighten my senses again, to bring me nearer the world once more; in my security I have forgotten how to dance."

In the connected, high-tech global world it is quite easy to forget the precarious precipice on which human life sits. Awesome acts of terrorism, despotism and genocide, earthquakes, tornadoes and floods, random acts of social violence, industrial and urban accidents and even recreational missteps can in an instance snuff the passions and hopes of people. One day we walk merrily through life, innocently assuming long tenure and a quiet death in a warm retirement villa, the next moment it is gone.

At extreme moments of natural and artificial disaster, it is compelling to think about the shortness of life, its precious gift and the need to live it moment by moment. In man's search for meaning, these events often serve to call attention to important areas of our lives we are ignoring or mishandling. Moments of disaster remind us that there are more important enterprises than the mindless pursuit of power, technical competence, fame and money – the insatiable and sometimes destructive system of progress and dominance that seems to generate only short-lived hits of pleasure – and often at the expense of others.

Every moment offers the opportunity to enjoy the splendour of the day's gift, the people around us and the simple contributions we have to make to them and the planet at large. *We do not know how much time we each have, but we can know that in every moment we are living good lives and making a difference.*

Using Entrepreneurship as a Healing Practice

I once rented a house built by an electrician.   It had no lights wired into the basement. This cliché comes in many forms – the shoemaker's children going without shoes – all speaking to the irony and need for us to teach what we need to learn, to work in an area and to choose a business that is a good arena for our personal growth.

I think that for whatever reason and no matter how severe, each person emerges from their childhood with some scrapes and bruises – some physical and others psychological. While certain children no doubt suffered more terrible abuses, I think we all had some wounding. Despite the best intentions of parents, friends, teachers and even society as a whole, we all collected our scars and disappointments from trying to adapt to a sometimes hostile world for which we did not have the understanding or skills to navigate with perfect grace. We can all use more love.

Enter Brian Paterson. Brian is a lawyer. With that introduction, Brian does not necessarily earn the respect and admiration of his audience. The practice of law and lawyers do not have a perfectly stellar reputation. There are hundreds of pejorative lawyer jokes and thousands of bad and exploitive lawyers that have given his field the often bad name it gets. But Brian is not just a lawyer, he is a holistic lawyer. He uses words like love and spirituality to describe his approach to the law – the higher law. While many of his counterparts view the law as an adversarial and litigious discipline, Brian views conflict as an opportunity for personal growth and for healing. He rarely litigates; he mediates and views any legal situation as a way to learn. The conflict's purpose is to teach us something about ourselves and about life – about the big picture. At some level, everything is perfect. And that is what makes him a holistic lawyer.

Randy Revell, one of the original innovators in the field of personal growth, often says "the calling springs forth from the wound." In other words, whatever pain we bring with us from childhood is what drives us to create value for other people. *We are motivated to serve others and create value simply because we have been hurt in the precise area in which we seek to make a difference.* It is our place of natural empathy. Brian, no doubt, experienced conflict and chaos in his youth and no doubt did not like the stress he experienced along with it. It is easy to see why he would be so passionate about helping people create love out of their conflicts. He is about love, the practice of law is his vehicle. As he creates this value for others, he heals himself. He is teaching what he himself needs to learn. This work is his calling and his path to wholeness.

One part of my business is about creating a better integration between entrepreneurs and their clients precisely because my parents did not create a working marriage. The disintegration of my family and the stress it caused are important parts of my personal history, galvanizing my commitment to building common ground. I was not an abused child, but my parents' divorce certainly shaped my calling to bring people together in a way that they did not themselves. I am grateful for the experience. Brian would say that I had the perfect parents to create the temperament I now draw from to accomplish my work. From the wound comes the celebration of creating value in that area. For me, disconnection is an opportunity, and the joy I see in it is the same joy Brian sees in conflict. There is something great in every malady, tragedy and stress. The Latin word for suffering is "passion." As we rise above our pain and stress, we capture the passion that drives our callings and experience the joy that comes from creating value. I think that is the point of being an entrepreneur.

Years ago, friends of mine went out on a long multi-day backpacking trip. Among the party of six hikers was one man who spent his evenings at camp giving all the other people in the party thorough foot massages. These were real treats at the end of long days spent pounding over roots and rocks and through swamps and unstable beach sand with heavy backpacks. As the days passed, the other hikers began taking items from this man's pack to lighten his load. During the final days, he enjoyed a whisper-light pack, while his compatriots shouldered his gear equally among them.

In *The Selfish Gene* evolutionary biologist Richard Dawkins, proposed the idea that the human biological system always acts in the interests of enhancing its survival prospects. Altruism, the apparent selfless giving from one to another, from this perspective, has some strategic merit. Contribution might be an adaptive behaviour evolved through natural selection. It is quite possible that the best strategy to take care of ourselves in a resource-competitive environment is to take care of those around us. As we invest ourselves in creating value for others, in working to enhance the experiences and results of our clients, in time our own experiences and results follow on. It pays to contribute.

As an entrepreneur and member of the famous Generation X, I have come to develop a different view of retirement. As trailing members of the baby boom, and born in the most prolific six year period of the boom at that, people in my age group faced stiff competition for university positions and first jobs. With bleak employment prospects, rising house prices and the threat of a bankrupt pension system, many of us became entrepreneurs and struck out on our own. Generation X became Generation E. As we have proceeded through our entrepreneurial careers, senior boomers have been chanting

"Freedom 55." Early retirement is quite possible for them, and perhaps desirable. They have profited from favourable economics, and many have jobs they hate, which they cannot wait to retire from. I am sure that members of my cohort did not want those jobs anyway. Instead, we embraced the concept of doing work we love. And when we are doing work we love, we tend not fantasize about the day when we no longer have to do it. That concept does not exist.

While financial independence is an interesting prospect, I have no plan to retire in the traditional sense. It seems fruitless to me to work like a dog for forty years, sacrificing my health and family, just to be "free" during my adult-diaper, kidney-dialysis years and end up dying bored before my time. I plan to do what I love my whole life and "retire" for a big chunk every year – while I am fit and my kids still want me around. I have already retired from working Wednesdays. This keeps my energy high for my clients, since I spend the middle day of the week recharging. I have an extra fifty-two days a year for reading, writing, climbing, dog sledding or whatever I feel like. I plan to keel over my laptop, on some beach, after I have just written a particularly satisfying piece of prose.

While I am still building my tax shelters and mutual funds, the primary instrument of my financial portfolio, and my ultimate path to financial independence, is the capacity of my business to generate repeat business and residual income. And this means always being conscious of the lifetime value of a customer. I invest considerable time, energy and money to enroll clients – my people – into my network. I have learned that my customers are not merely transactions but permanent, mutually-valuable relationships: people with a lifetime of needs and opportunities for me to serve. My purpose is to make a sustainable contribution to the quality of their lives until the end of mine. *As we grow as entrepreneurs and continue to support our people with valuable new innovations, they continue to support us with permanent streams of revenue.*

Maximizing Taxes and Maximizing Impact

Harry Taylor is a different sort of accountant – the first one I ever met who used the word "passion" to describe his practice. He also broke through another stereotype. Many accountants in public practice do tax work, specifically with the objective of minimizing the amount of taxes their clients pay. This can create savings many times over the fees they charge and make an investment into an accountant's services well worth the time, energy and money expended. The problem arises from taking tax minimizing to it ultimate fruition: minimal taxes result from minimal revenue and income on which to pay them. Minimizing taxes can suppress the growth of the enterprise.

As a young person and entrepreneur, I was taught to minimize the taxes I paid. I really bought into this as a wise business practice. Plus, as someone living in Western Canada, under an Eastern-biased Federal Government, I was quite happy at the thought of limiting the flow of my cash into that particular corporation. I saw the government as an unwanted business partner grabbing almost half of my profits without doing anything to earn them. They would only squander it anyway.

It turns out that I was grossly mistaken in holding these views, and for years I paid a steep price for them. Recently, I heard of an entrepreneur who limits his annual sales revenue to $30K; beyond that figure he would start having to pay GST. Of course this is fallacious reasoning, since above $30K he would simply have to charge a premium and then submit the proceeds. It would not really cost him anything and customers are accustomed to paying the tax anyway. Trying to avoid the 7% premium cost him something far more dear. The act of constraining his growth meant that he did not fulfill the increasing demand for his service. Competitors came in, and now he is unable to maintain even $30K in annual revenues. His business is shrinking, and it might now perish. I thought this scenario reflected quite odd thinking, until I realized that years ago I had decided to actively keep my personal taxable income to below a similar magic threshold.

I reasoned that above a certain level my taxes would increase and I would start taking less and less home. This of course meant that I had to also constrain my business sales. If I let my business become too big, then I would have to pay something more than the minimum tax load. In my zeal to limit my tax load, I was limiting my growth. I had actually made less money than I could have, and, even worse, I had capped my creative expression. Since that expression is how I make my money, as I constrained my sales, I constrained my expression.

What I did not understand is Harry's idea of paying as much tax as I could, that increased tax rates only apply to marginal increases in income. That was an important, though somewhat obvious insight. I was more focused on the 39 cents I would lose than by the 61 cents I would gain from each additional dollar of income. Since retaining him as my accountant, I am paying more taxes now. He is still diligent in applying the tax code fairly to my situation so I do not over pay, but I am making much more in sales and thus creating much more value.

Even at the higher tax brackets, I still keep most of what I earn, and I am never worse off for earning more profit. Also, I make a bigger difference by seeing myself as a country, province and city builder. It is true that governments squander money, but it is also true that taxes contribute to the quality of life, the built world and the environment. *If we were all paying more taxes, it would mean that we were creating more value and abundance for ourselves and the rest of the country.* As I take greater ownership over my taxes, I take greater ownership over my life.

Giving Away What We Need

When I was six years old, my mother discovered that I had a high need for acknowledgment. Unfortunately for her, and ultimately for me, that discovery was painful. My parents were very enterprising and busy. My family spent many weekends at the lakeside cottage of some close friends. One day I decided to hide from them under a bed and listened for hours, with perverse satisfaction, to everyone's frantic searching and increasing panic. Obviously my parents ran through the various scenarios – abduction, drowning, animal attack – and were relieved when I finally emerged. I had designed my behaviour to force my parents to acknowledge that I was special. This was obviously not a constructive behaviour. I got my need for acknowledgment met at their expense – and mine; I could not sit down for the rest of the weekend.

Everyone has a similar set of emotional needs. Their satisfaction represents our overall feeling of well-being. These needs are on a different plane than other baser requirements of life. In addition to material needs for food, water, shelter, comfort, security, we all have more spiritual needs – the experiences we crave in every moment in order to feel fulfilled. When I satisfy these driving needs constructively, life flows through me. Acknowledgment is not unlike the needs other people have for attention, recognition, appreciation, respect, validation, consideration, expression, distinction, honour, clarity, certainty or peace. I have driving needs also for passion, power and connection, which have their analogs in experiences like excitement, fun, drama, adventure, discovery, diversity, freedom, control, intimacy, belonging, harmony, loyalty, trust, security, commitment, dedication and confidence.

Learning to fulfill our emotional needs constructively and actively is a process of mastery and increasing consciousness. The need for acknowledgment is the emotional need to be heard and to feel special. The question then arises, who is the proper source of acknowledgment in my life?

I sometimes see other people as the source of my satisfaction. This happens when I get acknowledgment from people. This way of satisfying needs while not destructive, is not really constructive either. It is passive. I sit back and let the world come to me with its praises. The problem with this approach is that I give my power away to forces outside of me, who do not always have my best interests at heart. If the praise does not come, I start to feel empty and often resort to destructive behaviour. We are accustomed to thinking that someone else ought to supply what we need. We learned shortly after birth to cry and someone came rushing to figure out what was wrong and fixed it. As adults, we can drift back to this more archaic approach. It does not, ultimately, work well.

I take the position that I am the source of my own experience, and I see my business as the source of a positive experience for others. This means that in relationship to my people, whether family, clients or friends, I become the source of acknowledgment. *Ironically, it is more fulfilling to give away what we ourselves need because it requires that we take action to constructively create the same experiences that we want from others.* As I hear others, I satisfy my own need to be heard. As I help other people see what is special about them, I come to appreciate that ability as what is special about me.

This is a leap of faith and takes much practice. As I own the idea that I am the source of the fulfilling experiences I seek, I take the control I always had and create them at will for me and the people I most care about. The question "what can I give you?" takes me further along in business and life than "how can you satisfy my needs?"

When my brother and I were in our teens, our mother started a retail business. Her esthetics shop offered women a variety of products and services, like manicures and pedicures and all manner of creams and other things centered around the idea of "feminine artistry." We would spend time down at the shop and observed how business was done. As she was performing various services for clients, I watched my mother "sell" the other merchandise that would naturally accompany the services. My mother or one of her colleagues and a client would be engaged in an interesting conversation, and, somehow, by the end they had done business. To me, the conversation appeared to have nothing to do with the stuff in the jars or the other services on the rate sheet, it just seemed to be about the things women liked to talk about. Then at the end of the service, the customer would get up and go over to the register and buy a whole bunch of things, charging a whopping amount on her Visa card. The transaction took place, but if I did stop-motion video analysis of the procedure, I would have been mystified to find the exact "moment of the close."

There are few things that stress out and strike fear in the hearts of most service providers as much as selling. To sell, one must risk rejection and the recrimination of a society that equates selling with evil, coercive, lowlife bottom feeders. Service providers can learn a lot from retailers. Unlike other service providers, whose product is their time, retailers get paid out of the gross margin, reselling items they have bought from manufacturers. They need double the sales to make the same money as other professionals. Thus retailers have conquered many of the stigmas of selling.

I have since watched dozens of great retailers engaged in great conversations with people, and the business just seems to happen. Conversation is probably the feminine gift to business. That it started in retail is not a great surprise, because years ago, low paying retail jobs were one of only a few places that women could work. Traditionally, girls were brought up to relate, talk and discuss feelings. This was foreign to many boys in my generation. We grew up playing war with guns or in competitive win-lose sports. There was always an enemy that required defeat. During the past fifty years, many men took this approach into the selling world, giving the profession the bad name it now holds. Selling became a competitive win-lose sport, with a prospect that required defeat. The moment of close, was for many male sales reps, the moment that the dagger struck the heart.

People generally love to buy but hate to be sold. In the best stores, customers buy and the store does not push the sale. Retailers of course need to sell to maintain a healthy business, but they genuinely love people. Pushy sales people get screened out with Darwinian efficiency. In the best, high-end retail situations, employees are surely trained in the techniques of rapport building, presentation, objection handling and closing, but the best ones have an art for conversation. They are genuinely interested in people and what they have to say.

A good conversation encourages personal expression. Since purchasing is also an exercise in personal expression, especially in high-end purchases where the person is not acquiring a commodity item, a good conversation encourages the purchase as well. Conversation loosens suppressed emotions and generates interest – two elements of any successful high-margin sale. Selling is still a process of making agreement with another person to exchange cash for a product. Good sales people never lose sight of that reality, it is just not their only reality. *Conversation is a great way to learn about people, to discuss different points of view and to ultimately reconcile them in the form of a high-end purchase.*

Learning to Appreciate What Appreciates

When my brother and I were growing up, our mother always encouraged us to invite our stranded friends to holiday dinners. Whether it was for Christmas or Thanksgiving, anyone who had no where else to go was welcome at her table. We would only have to arrive home with someone unannounced and she would set another place at the table, squeezing a chair, plate and utensils into an already crowded banquet. Our family bulged at the various holidays. Whether the participants were related to us was irrelevant to her. When they spent time in my mother's home they felt welcome and even though they were not able to go home for the holidays, they felt at home. That spirit of welcoming is one of the values she stands for and it is the guiding principle behind her generosity and her sense of community.

Growing up in that kind of environment, we gained an appreciation for friends, family and the value of good relationships. Even in business, many years later, I have learned that marketing is really just a community building endeavour: make connections with different kinds of people, treat them well, be generous and the business part takes care of itself. Wealth need not be forced, it flows from good re-lationships.

My mother has enterprising attitude and I am grateful for her example. Now retired, she was part of a successful, professional apartment-hotel business and created a loyal and lucrative community of customers. She created millions of dollars of revenue for her company. All of this resulted from her spirit of generosity. My mother loves people. Whether she was on the phone with a prospective client, checking in a new one or arranging for the special requirements of a long-standing guest, everyone felt welcome "at her table." Her sense of spirit drove her revenue. It worked because clients felt genuinely appreciated. Her people repaid her generous service with their loyalty and repeat business. Because she stands for generosity, gratitude is a constant undertone in everything she does. The better she treated people, the more they felt welcome and the bigger her network became. What she gave to people, always seemed to come back to her, many times over. She leaves a rich legacy of strong relationships and good karma that her former company will benefit from for years to come.

Gratitude works for two reasons. First, it honors the people in our lives who are good to us. Second, since gratitude as a process is the acknowledgment of what is good, being grateful is a way for us to connect with and honor our own good. As I am acknowledging the good outside of me, it creates more space to acknowledge the good inside of me. If it is true that other people are a mirror for me, then the good that I see in them, reflects the good that I carry in me. Gratitude is good for the people I appreciate, for me and for my business.

Giving thanks is a way for us to honour the people who participate in our personal lives and business ventures and to strengthen the community of supporters who are vested in our best interests. I am grateful for the people who have joined and have stayed a part of my community. I am grateful for my friends, family and allies out there, who have been a part of my life and vision and have stood by me during the marching on of the years, through innumerable moments of support. I am grateful for all of my clients, old and new, who have bought in and supported my business and its many experiments. I am grateful for the curiosity of the people who are just getting to know me. I am grateful to my father for his adventuous spirit. And I am grateful to my mother for her generosity and fine example of always treating people the way they best deserved to be treated.

Moving Back Into Abundance

Many of us struggle with the dance between scarcity and abundance. Scarcity comes as a result of many different kinds of beliefs. Sometimes it finds direct expression in the thought that "there is not enough to go around" and in indirect thoughts like "it has to look a certain way", "if someone else wins I can't", "I am not good enough the way I am", "I am only worth this much" or "I can't have everything I want or need." These are crippling thought patterns that suppress the feeling of being alive and connected in every moment. Most people have some version of these beliefs.

I believe that the root of scarcity lies in the misunderstanding that abundance is some long away future result, some sort of mythical, defining moment of success that happens to us if and when we are deserving of it. Everyone has some sort of set-point, limiting the amount of good fortune that comes their way. Good fortune is a very direct reflection of the esteem we feel and the sense of worth we choose. While a small few rise above the crowd of more impoverished souls, the bulk of humanity lives some form of capped existence. I think we owe this to thousands of years of religious precedent that prescribed an ascetic life of sacrifice in order to earn the wealth of heaven and parents who were born before the War and who learned to squirrel away their cash.

A more Postmodern concept of abundance is not strictly financial and not strictly about results. Abundance, from this perspective is a process. It is not something we work towards, but a natural state we were born with, a default state. If we are not experiencing abundance, then we have actually learned to work hard to stay in scarcity. Abundance from this point of view is easier.

Abundance is flow. Energy, joy, passion, beauty, love, connection and contribution are the stuff of abundance. It is through sharing these that we experience abundance. Like any flow state, abundance has an input and output. We create scarcity when we overemphasize the input function of "getting" and underemphasize the output function of "giving."

Scarcity often comes as the result of hoarding behaviours borne of some fear of loss. It stifles sharing and perpetuates the fear of scarcity, which drove the hoarding in the first place. This belief blocks the output, raising the pressure in the system and preventing anything else from entering. Ironically, the path back into a state of flow is one of spending. Spending myself in the pursuit of contribution and enjoyment empties the output. This act of giving creates a vacuum in the energy flow so that more of what I spent flows back in.

We tap into abundance by activating the three temporal senses of flow: past, present and future. The first spending mode honors our debts to the past. This literally means paying off our financial debts. It also means providing for others who need our support: creating value for clients, raising our families, taking care of parents, maintaining loving friendships and helping to make life work for the billions of people who are struggling just to keep their families fed and rain off of their heads. In this way, we show appreciation for the countless souls who passed before, and created the opportunities that we now exploit. The second spending mode celebrates the joys of the present. In this mode, we enjoy the full portfolio of experiences and things life has to offer, using our resources to surround ourselves with beauty and engage our passions. The third mode of spending is our investment in future visions that amplify the flow, lever our resources, secure our slower retirement days and assure that we are always able to pay for the past and present.

Spending and not hoarding whatever it is we want more of puts us back into the natural flow of what was, what is and what will be.

Economic Value Added   87
Expanding the Problem Space to Create More Value

Economic-value-added (EVA) is the measurement of residual or accumulated wealth created in an enterprise. Also known as economic profit, it refers to the retained earnings or cumulative profit less a charge for capital costs. As the authors of the book *EVA* have pointed out, to gauge the true financial success of a venture, entrepreneurs must factor in the cost of all capital, not just debt. Thus if you invest a lifetime of energy, time and money into your venture, resources that you could have allocated elsewhere, the cost of that allocation needs to be reflected in the measurement. In other words, we all need to place a value on the energy, time and money we invest in our own businesses and factor in the opportunity cost to help us focus on creating real wealth.

For entrepreneurs, EVA is a crucial metric simply because, for many of us, our businesses are our greatest assets and our retirement funds. This is important to acknowledge because service businesses that charge by the hour may not build up any of this residual value. Residual value creates passive income and is easy to measure since it is what we earn when we are not actually working.

EVA may be our objective in business, but it is not our purpose. The purpose of a service business is to create value for other human beings. In a service business, the essence of such value is not financial but personal. It is the creation of something important, in collaboration with team members and paying clients. Personal-value-added (PVA) precedes EVA (accumulated profit.)

Solving problems is the basis of all value creation. Everyone has problems. Some problems are mild irritants which people are quite capable of solving on their own. Others require professional intervention. In the user-domain of a business, the client or user experiences some kind of stress. The service and product exist to relieve this stress. The product solves a very specific problem of particular importance to the user.

In my business, I solve four kinds of problems: confusion, indifference, overwhelm and conflict. These stresses reflect the need for certain kinds of value: authenticity, contribution, elegance and integration. In the delivery of my product, I work with my clients to create these values. When we co-create the value of contribution or making a bigger difference, we remove the stress of indifference. Indifference is what my clients experience when their prices and margins are too low and when they work only to deliver the technical commodity and fail to express the special value inside. Clients just do not care that much about a technical commodity. The problem is that the entrepreneurs have not fully integrated their core values into their product design and into the choice of their clients.

As we commit to making a bigger difference, our offerings become more valuable to more valuable customers who become passionate about the product. Passionate clients pay more and so both margins increase. With more cashflow, we are free to make an even bigger difference and experience even greater passion. Passion is what someone experiences in the presence of contribution, while indifference is what they experience in its absence. The more contribution we create, the more passion our clients experiences and the more they pay. If we wish to create higher prices and higher margins we need to create more PVA; we need to create more of all of our core values, experiences and results for our own clients.

Stress indicates an opportunity to create value. The bigger the stress, the bigger the opportunity. *As we continue to expand the problem space, finding ever more complex and stressful situations to solve, we earn higher pay as our share of the greater results we generate by solving them.*

It is possible to increase profit by increasing volume, raising prices and lowering cost, but as service providers, raising prices is the most interesting approach. Increasing volume requires work to expand the scale of a venture, either because we lengthen our work weeks or add the complexities of managing staff. Lowering costs is a poor choice because there is a limit as to how much we can or would even want to pare down, since our costs tend to be made up of sales and marketing expenditures which bring in more revenue, wages which we take home for living and administration which includes the comforts of offices and the fun technical equipment we use.

When I was a young product designer, my company was charged with the development of a computerized baby bassinet. The product had a rhythmic motion which helped colicky and upset babies to sleep. A marketing consultant we were working with measured price sensitivity by interviewing prospective customers in both Northern and Southern California. We measured two retail price-points, $249 and $189, and discovered that parents were almost equally likely to purchase at either price. This made sense: if a baby was keeping you up all night and was degrading the quality of your marriage and work-life, you would want the product almost regardless of price.

This was from the start a high-value-adding product: it offered clear and important results. Based on the statistics gathered, we recommended retailing the product at $249 through the network of boutique stores across North America. These retailers would and could, by virtue of the margins we offered, afford to support the product with the level of front-line service this kind of product needed and deserved. However, our client was a public company and needed hype and rapid growth to drive up the stock price. Thus the retail focus changed from service-oriented boutiques to no-service mass-merchants. Instead of offering the product at $249, the venture capitalists and retail buyers forced the price-point down to $99, closer in price to wicker bassinets.

This sales tactic immediately killed consumers' perception of value and prompted a high-pressure cost reducing exercise. The product cost about $60 to make at volume, which provided ample margins through the boutiques selling at $249 but no margin for anybody through mass-merchants. It did not take long for poor sales support, insufficient marketing and negative margins to kill an otherwise promising high-value product. Increasing volumes only sped its demise, and there was a natural limit to how much cost could be stripped out, while maintaining the integrity and safety of the original concept. Only value-based pricing would have worked in this case.

High-value, premium products command premium prices. In a commodity marketplace of undifferentiated products, where price is the only difference amongst faceless competitors, customers search for the lowest possible price. Prospects view the prices of any commodity as an expense and any price, no matter how low is "expensive." High-value items are investments that provide a return.

Value-based pricing requires that we consider the customer's profit through tangible, measurable results. By making a transition in our own thinking from "how much does it cost?" to "how much is the return?" we naturally create a more valuable offer and conversation. By attending to our client's need for a return on their service investment, we create a product that delivers that return. *A service that returns many times its price back in tangible, measurable results is an investment that justifies a higher price, not an expense that prompts price objections.* This means basing the price of our services on the results we create, rather than on how much time it took to create them. High prices are the economic representation of important results.

Value-added-resellers (VARs) are an invention of the computer industry. Value-added-resellers package a low-margin com-modity, such as computer hardware, with higher-margin services such as installation and training. The whole becomes greater than the sum of the parts and results in a higher total price. There are three main ways to determine the price for any product or service. The first, cost-line billing, is to mark-up the cost of services. The second, market-rate billing, is to set prices within range of competitors. The third, value-billing, is to allow prices to reflect the important results and experiences that clients receive. The "internal" hourly rate and what competitors charge become less relevant. We can charge more money by creating more value.

I first learned this concept as a product development consultant. We built an extensive network of Asian man-ufacturers that could build products fast, well and for prices much lower than their North American competitors. One client, after scouring this continent for quotes on plastic molds asked us to source an Asian supplier. The best price onshore was $300K with a lead-time of 16 weeks. My source could provide good quality in 8 weeks for $100K, a substantial savings in both time and money. This was an opportunity to package our high-margin design and engineering services with the sourcing service that would save them many times our fees. If we had just sold the sourcing information to the client and charged a typical hourly rate for the brief time it took to pass it on, it would have dishonoured the equity we had built up in our network.

The practice of law offers great scope for value-added-reselling. Customers are not always elated about receiving a bill from their lawyer. An invoice from a typical law firm has entries like, "attend upon the matter of the discovery: 55

minutes x $250/hour", "telephone conference with client: 10 minutes x $250/hour", "transcribe conference minutes: 20 minutes x $100/hour", "5 photocopies x 25¢/copy" and "one facsimile transmission: $5/page." These "nickel and dime" billings are cost-line and market-rate invoices that annoy many people and make it tempting to think: "Did he really spend ten minutes on the phone with me or was it really five?" Working in five or sixty minute increments overshadows real results, important to real people using real cash to settle the bill. Lawyers are talented and creative people who provide entrepreneurs with much more value than their commodities and commodity-pricing suggest.

A typical legal commodity is the incorporation of a company. Some lawyers have the price of this down to $200 but they miss the true opportunity. New entrepreneurs need more at the start of their ventures than a minute book and a certificate that allows them to open a bank account. The failure rates of new business starts are notoriously high. What a new venture needs is the best possible start. Defining the issue as an incorporation problem is a disservice to the client and does nothing to allay the risks and perils of launch. A better problem definition is to see the situation as a capital structure and risk management project. The lawyer could package a number of services to support a start-up in negotiating the early phases of its life. People might appreciate an invoice that reflects results worth many times the amount, like: "$5,000 to create an effective business structure in which everyone is free to contribute their best creative efforts and is paid a fair split of the proceeds and no one wanders off with your ideas or other assets." If people risk losing their life savings going out of business, they might prefer spending an additional $4800 to assure that they do not. *An integrated service program is a package of solutions that has greater value than time sold by the hour.*

Making the Act of Choosing No Penance

The phrase "what goes around, comes around" aptly describes most people's notion of karma. Karma is a Sanskrit word denoting the sum of a person's attitudes and thoughts that determine their place in the next round of life, for better or worse. Karma is a central tenet in the idea of reincarnation. Now, whether one believes in reincarnation or not, the karma meme has invaded popular culture and finds application not just in the life to life sense but in the moment to moment sense within a particular person's lifetime.

Another way to understand the notion of karma is through the concept of the self-fulfilling prophecy, illustrated by Napoleon Hill's idea that whatever the mind believes, it can achieve. In practical terms, karma means that the thought precedes the deed – as we think, so we become. Good comes from good will, and bad from ill will.

Many children experience high expectations from their parents. In biological-evolutionary terms, parents sometimes hope their children live a better life than they did, that the children do not make the same mistakes. Parents want to pass on their wisdom of how to live a productive life so that their progeny might thrive. Thriving is a good thing in Darwinian terms. Parents and society as a whole have instilled in the child, along with the program of hopes and dreams, a natural guilt mechanism: fail to conform to their expectations, commit a sin against the standard of good and it is easy to feel bad and worthless.

Penance is a term that describes the punishment someone must do in order to make up for the commission of some sin. When we decide to do penance for any reason, we are less likely to bring good outcomes into our lives.

It is well-contended in personal growth circles that people are their own greatest enemies, that they have a well-developed arsenal of self-sabotaging beliefs and behaviours. Applied to the problem of enterprise, it is the entrepreneurs that must overcome their own patterns of self-destruction to achieve success. The personal growth of an entrepreneur is therefore all about the systematic transformation of belief and behaviour systems from those that do not work to those that do. A venture built on such worthy practices becomes a healthy, thriving venture in much the same way that a child becomes a healthy, thriving person.

Dharma is another Sanskrit term that denotes the essential good purpose that lies within someone. Dharma is what anchors our core values to the conscious action of contributing to others and the greater good. When karma and dharma find their alignment, a stream of good flows out. When these forces are at work there is no guilt in following one's dharma or sense of life mission because of its intrinsic value and place within us as our driving force. This leads to good karma.

When we fail to conform to external standards we might experience guilt and consequently set up "bad karma." At this time a person might choose to do penance for the sin of not conforming to the expectations of parents and society, and thereby invite the misery of failure to come calling. And it does come calling. Then we respond, "It serves me right; I deserve this."

Such is the power of a negative self-fulfilling prophecy. Of course, the opposite is true. Changing our minds from bad to good is just as powerful. *By refusing to do penance for sins against standards we do not choose as our own, we set forth a powerful mechanism of goodwill that invites all manner of prosperity and good times.* Then we can all say, "It serves me right; I deserve this."

Anyone who knows me well, knows that I love shoes. It seems I am not alone. The Beaverton, Oregon based company Nike has become the premier global brand in this area. This means that millions of the citizens on this planet identify with and buy into what Nike is all about. Zealots tattoo the swoosh logo onto their bodies or shave it onto their heads. The other purchasers advertise the logo on their shoes, apparel, luggage, posters and other "artifacts." Synonymous with "victory", the Nike brand is arguably the most valuable asset of the company, particularly because the company does not really make or sell their product. The shoes are not necessarily better than other shoes, but they mean more to more people who buy them.

Nike is a profitable company. I used to regularly purchase Nike shoes and garments, and I have come to respect many facets of the way they do business. I ceased purchasing Nike goods when I discovered a Jim Collins article in *Inc.* magazine that described their core purpose, "to experience the emotion of competition, winning and crushing competitors." This put words to an uneasy feeling I had as their customer. One part of the company I did not respect was their weed-like global growth pattern and their seeming willingness to do anything to capture new markets and crush the incumbent suppliers in the market space. I identified with their nobler view of competition, the idea of the best athletes pushing each other to greatness in a spectacular foot race, but the company now seemed to be taking on the tenor of the global bully.

There are many people who criticize others for being "brand-conscious." Perhaps it is a residue of the previous decade of conspicuous consumption where people did try to "purchase" happiness and self-esteem. I am confident that a brand is not a replacement for my self-esteem. It can, however, be a celebration of my self-esteem, a tribute to what I am passionate about.

While I am no longer a particularly passionate customer of Nike, I am a loyal follower of a once obscure and presently deceased foot surgeon by the name of Salvatore Ferragamo. Salvatore lived in Italy near the turn of the last century and humbly founded one of the great fashion empires. The Ferragamos are one of Italy's wealthiest families, and I am quite certain I know how they got there.

Nine years ago, I was about to participate in my first consumer products trade show in Dallas, Texas. After the first day, my client made a "supportive suggestion" that I upgrade my business shoes. I was not long out of university, and so I had not indulged this part of my wardrobe. I purchased a new pair of shoes by Cole Haan, now a part of the Nike empire, and suffered painful feet for the remaining days of the show.

The year after, I found myself at the same tradeshow, in need of another pair of shoes, and then in a Neiman Marcus shoe department in Dallas ready to repeat what seemed to be a new tradition. The sales person started by telling me the Ferragamo story. Ferragamo was a progressive doctor who had invented a unique set of shoe molds, based on an astute understanding of proper walking and standing posture. I appreciate this sort of heritage and fell in love with the company even before I had the shoes on my feet. I slipped them on and felt like a god the whole week.

People are creatures of meaning. Purchasing is a meaningful act of self-expression. *As consumers, we reward companies which reflect our values and offer meaningful products and services by paying premium prices and remaining loyal.* The wealthiest companies are also the most meaningful. They have the strongest brands. Meaning works. It works for Nike. It works for Ferragamo.

In our current economy, the word innovation most often connotes high tech. But innovation is not merely a technical process, the invention of something new and the discovery and synthesis of new knowledge. Innovation is also a social phenomenon, the full fruition of an invention. An innovation is an invention that has achieved full penetration and diffusion throughout a community.

There are some people within these communities who buy-in before others. This is the classic diffusion-of-innovation curve, a bell curve that essentially reflects a population's varying sensitivity to new technology and ideas. In *Crossing the Chasm*, Geoffrey Moore speaks of the gap that any new idea must cross to reach its full potential, from the smaller early market to the larger primary market. There are two basic kinds of clients making up each side of the chasm: those who believe it before they see it and those who need to see it before they believe it: the visionaries and the pragmatists. The gap exists because there is a much smaller proportion of visionaries in any new market and pragmatists are unimpressed by the fact that some visionary has bought into a new program.

Visionaries and Pragmatists adopt new ideas for entirely different reasons. While visionaries are content to take a leap of faith, pragmatists prefer to see a credible track record of results before they buy. Pragmatists are more numerous and thus constitute the majority of eventual sales.

The penetration of a new market space requires credibility with an ever larger and more doubtful audience. I once met a very successful product design consultant in Ottawa. His first "client" and "project" was to build a deck for his neighbour, hardly what he had acquired an expensive design education for. He had no portfolio showing the pictures of successful products he had designed and so this was the best first paying job he could find. But he did a great job on the deck and the neighbour introduced him to a local manufacturer who did not have a big budget or an exciting project but who was willing to take a chance. From there he was referred up the chain to more exciting, sophisticated and better paying work. Within five years he had a great portfolio, a large staff and was working for premium clients like Black and Decker and Northern Telecom on exciting design problems for premium fees. He had crossed the chasm and had signed up the most conservative and most lucrative purchasers of design services. It was not until this designer had a proven track record – credibility from having successfully served some of the more daring pragmatists – that the rest of pragmatic buyers thought it was safe to buy.

Brian Tracy proposed that the best prospects do not buy from the vendor with the lowest prices but from vendors who offer the least risk. This means that fear of loss is a powerful motivator. As we move up the echelons of ever-sophisticated clients and projects we inevitably build credibility – documented proof of success which mitigates the fear and risk. Of course, innovation is about doing things that have never been done before and is a process that begins by making new offers to new prospects with whom there is no track record.

It is during these times of aspiration towards new heights of creation that we need something in the stead of material credibility, to calm the fear and risk. That is confidence: the simple faith in our ability to create something of value for a new level of client, in spite of having no material evidence to support such a claim. *It is confidence – our spiritual connection to our creativity – that is the precondition of creating the successful track record that most clients need before buying in to something new.* Our belief in the possibility must always preexist the eventual success. As we believe, so can our new clients believe. Confidence allows us to venture into the creative abyss of innovation and confidence makes it safe for our best clients to follow.

Overcoming the Cult of Technology

The design school I attended was part of an environmental design faculty that strongly promoted the idea of interdisciplinary team work. One aspect of this was a substantial grounding in ergonomics and human factors, the science of creating a productive interface between a product and the people that would come to use it. Part of my schooling was a one year practicum at a local design firm. This firm was itself interdisciplinary and had many kinds of engineers and researchers in addition to industrial designers. I observed firsthand the challenges of making new, highly technical products work for the people who were using them.

One project the company was working on was a custom-designed wheel chair for a young man severely disabled by spina bifida. He had never had a new chair, much less a chair designed for him, and was always excited every time he visited the studio. "New chair, new chair!" he would always chant as he left the building, carried down the stairs by the folks taking care of him.

The engineers took what appeared to be an overly sophisticated approach to the design of the chair. I got the impression that they were more enthralled by the prospects of advancing technology than they were concerned about the person who would spend his life in the device. They built prototype after prototype, all of which failed to work. This process went on for months and still the young man maintained his enthusiasm. Finally, after eighteen fruitless months of technical development, the young man died. The biggest deal in his short life was this new chair, and he never got to sit in it and make it run. It was a heartbreaking tragedy to witness and impressed upon on me the utter failure of a purely high-tech approach to anything that needs to be even remotely human.

John Naisbitt coined the phrase "high tech, high touch" to denote the balance that must be struck between the technical and human dimension of products. Years later, with a design firm of my own, I was invited by a venture capitalist to participate in the design of a new product for the disabled market. The company was Madenta Technologies which supported people with many sorts of interesting disabilities. Its leader Randy Marsden was committed to the concept of "enabling extraordinary people to do ordinary things." He had a respectful, high-touch, approach to people and technology.

Randy had been importing an American device called the "Headmouse" that allowed quadriplegics to use a computer. This product used infrared technology to track head movements and convert them into cursor movements. The American device was clunky, expensive to import and literally had to be duct taped onto a wheel chair. Madenta had managed to create a strong presence in the assistive technology market space and set about to develop its own product.

Madenta's original concept was an evolutionary improvement over the competition. My group refused to take on the job until Madenta conducted a user survey to find out what real people really wanted. Madenta resisted the idea at first. They were already close to their customers and were well acquainted with user needs, but they eventually agreed to bring users more directly into the design process. This is where they found out that people in wheel chairs often felt stigmatized by the technical, kludged-on products they got. They wanted something cool that no one else had. That insight led to a sleek, well-integrated product that set this group of users apart without alienating them. The revolutionary device went on to win international design recognition and assisted Madenta in capturing a large majority share of the market with an efficiently-produced, high-margin product. *Well-designed products and services balance the latest in technological advances with the very personal needs of the human beings using them.*

Breathing Life into a Business

In every discipline and walk of life, from hard-core quantum physics and cosmology, to medicine and entertainment, people are grappling with spirituality. Shunned during the 1980's consumerism and forsaken as quaint mythology, spirituality and faith are not necessarily part of the "new age" movement and neither are they necessarily religious notions, although they could be for some. Faith and spirit speak to basic life questions of purpose and meaning – the same questions Plato and Aristotle grappled with.

It is very interesting for entrepreneurs to talk about the pursuit of their spiritual callings. A business, from this perspective is not just a vehicle to earn a living, something to house a technology or a way to escape traditional employment. It is more than that. An enterprise is a vehicle for me to use my talent and express my faith in the service of other people, contributing to some of the important problems of the world. This is more interesting than a mere a profit motive. I am spiritual and my business is spiritual to the extent to which I honour my faith.

When I was in design school, I read the design philosophy of Ettore Sottsass, the acclaimed Italian designer, who proclaimed that "design is about life." It has taken me ten years to grok what that meant. I went into design school to learn how to make and sell products. I thought that it was commerce and money that drove designers and entrepreneurs. I was not at the place in life where I understood this ethereal phrase, but it whispered something important and profound.

As both an experienced consumer and entrepreneur, I have observed that there are two kinds of business: those that possess vitality and feel good when I am in their presence and those that do not. The word "vitality" finds its Latin roots in life, as "sustaining or essential to life". Reworking Sottsass, I could say that "business is about life." What this means to me is that businesses that have life, inspire people to feel good. They are full of spirit. The word spirit also has Latin roots: "to breathe." What is it, then, that is breathed into a business to give it life?

A sense of deep purpose gives business its life. It is an inspiring dialog between founders and customers about the meaning of life, what is truly important in life, what life is really about. At some level a business is a very basic transaction. Someone has a problem and some money; someone else has a solution and a desire for the money. They trade. At a grander level, it is a celebration of being alive, an exploration of the vibrant aesthetic splendour available to the senses and a way for human beings to connect. It could be about artistic expression, human achievement, discovery and curiosity, compassion and adversity, family and friendship, survival and abundance, nature and environment. When a business creates such a conversation, it transcends the material realities of doing business, just as humanity transcends its perfunctory operations of eating, sleeping, procreating, and keeping warm. It has risen above the short-term issues of technology, products and systems. People have animated the structure and it has come alive.

Most people acknowledge that there is more to life than meets the eye. I wonder about life, even as I am caught up in the struggle just to hold onto it. There is something deeply intriguing about being alive, just as there is something deeply intriguing about every entrepreneur who seeks to answer the calling they hear deep inside. *The most vital businesses rise above the technicalities of their operations to engage people in a deeper conversation about what matters most in life and the enterprise of making their way in the world.* Material realities are short-term realities. Spirit lasts forever.

What motivates people to create a venture, to work in its production, to finance its operations, to buy its products? The motive force driving all that commitment and action is the emotional content of the business. From Latin, "emotion" is what brings something to motion, to action. The emotive dimension of the venture is what makes it rich and compelling.

What marks the premium performers in any creative endeavour is their ability to translate and transpose the emotional aspect of life through their chosen media as an aesthetic experience. There are some media in which this is seemingly easier to do, or at least its result is more obvious. Great films, great acting, great music and poetry, great dance, great painting and sculpture, great design and architecture are aesthetic pursuits that move people. They seem to pursue and then capture the human spirit, allowing their audience to live the emotional experience.

The finest works of any art evoke the most visceral response in the audience: the tragic characters in film or on stage, rendered by actors who bring us to tears; standing in bewildered awe in the living area of Frank Lloyd Wright's "Falling Water" country home deftly perched atop a mountain stream in rural Pennsylvania; the cutting blues riffs of Colin James driving thousands of fans to rave in unison; the almost impossibly beautiful and delicate silk fabrics of Italian designers that appear as if they have been taken from watercolours of the Italian country side; novels which bring the page alive with stark and severe characters; the profound lyrics of great song writers; the voices of singers who carry us upward with the reach of single notes; the classic curve of a Porsche 911; an epicurean meal of carefully crafted scents and secret flavours; paintings and sculpture that transport us back to times past. These are not just articles of manufacture. They are products of profound human creation. They transcend the human experience and touch us where our souls are. They emote and provoke.

The aesthetic experience is not reserved for the the traditional arts or for the consumption of physical items from industry. There is an opportunity to evoke such poignant reactions from things quite technical and seemingly mundane: websites, e-commerce, and even things like legal and accounting services. This means seeing any technical endeavour for more than it literally is, just as poetry is more than words, music is more than notes on a page and acting is more than reciting lines from a script. In the classic arts, the practitioners have learned to integrate the discourse about life and its emotional content into their objects of creation. They have done so over centuries of practice and refinement, with the subtleties passed on through generations of master and protégé relationships. Our information-age businesses, scarcely a few decades old are lacking this depth of passion and tradition, but we can start the craft now.

The best businesses have always operated on the emotional plane. They see their role as solving a problem and removing stress – negative emotions – by adding value, creating a solution and delivering a positive experience – positive emotions. This works because at the highest level, the purchase and use of any service or product, especially the premium ones, are emotional activities. They are passionate. The features and underlying technology are there to facilitate the emotional process. They are justification after the fact of creating and connecting to the inspiring, authentic value lying within any great human artifice. *The more we reflect emotional content – the authentic aesthetic value – in every detail of our ventures, the more people are moved to buy, invest in, be a part of and use what we offer.*

Creating Lasting Memories for Customers

On the evening of our fifth wedding anniversary, my wife and I checked in to the Banff Springs Hotel. That evening was the very same day I gave the eulogy for Karl Nagy, a mountain guide and best friend. We arrived, caught between the tension of two opposing emotions, and the people at the Springs made a stunning experience for us that we will not forget. I vowed to make this the standard site for our anniversary celebrations, important occasions and other special rites of passage.

The Fairmont Banff Springs Hotel, has long been considered a jewel of Canadian history and tourism. The "Castle of the Rockies" is a national historical site and was one of the major focal points for the sweeping vision of William Van Horne, the commandant of the Canadian Pacific Railway, charged in the late 1800s with linking the bifurcated Canada with a smooth rail artery.

The contemporary Fairmont Hotel system split recently from the traditional Canadian Pacific corporation. The new entity holds the precious mission of providing guests with the remarkable experience of lasting memories, a legacy of Van Horne himself, who proclaimed with the opening of the hotel in 1888, that: "if we can't export the scenery, we will import the tourists."

I am writing these words in the grandeur of the Presidential Suite, as I overlook the stunning view of the Cascade range between the mountains Tunnel and Rundle, above the confluence of the Spray and Bow Rivers. I am here on the invitation of Michelle Nuyten, a hotel manager, as polite and generous compensation for a previous visit that fell short of her standards, the hotel's and ours. Just weeks after the 9-11 terrorist attacks, and on the occasion of our succeeding anniversary celebration, we checked into the hotel once more. Indeed, the world had tangibly shifted as a result of the horrific incident, and this was felt as a rippling aftershock in the hospitality industry. From the moment we arrived during this trip, the experience was off. I was so disappointed that I made a communication to the hotel, with the intention of preserving our tradition of great experiences. Michelle, who has a reputation for dazzling people, met me with an open ear, an accountable attitude and a vow to earn back our trust and respect.

I have had so many strongly-positive experiences here that it was hard to imagine being surprised in any way. While hotel management had offered a room for the weekend in exchange for the opportunity to make amends, I was expecting only a standard room. I appreciated the elegance of the gesture: the marginal cost of giving away a room that was unreserved anyway is small, the hotel would make a tidy margin from our restaurant activities and we would have a pleasant weekend retreat. Everyone would win. I was, nevertheless, unable to wipe a very dopey smile from my face while trying to keep my jaw from dropping to the floor as we were led up to the best room in the house. Champagne and birthday surprises were awaiting my wife, as were hand written notes of welcome from the hotel's senior managers and passes to the spa and valet parking.

It seems fitting that I am now in the throes of imprinting another such powerful and lasting memory into the history of my own life. While not the final chapter in the book, this is the last one I chose to write and I am pleased to be writing it in the rarefied air of the hotel's summit. Every time I will hold this book in my own hands, I will remember this day – the day I celebrated the end of a very long journey and the day that marked the start of a new one. My faith is indeed restored. Great companies make errors just as the merely good ones and poor ones do. *Greatness comes not from an absence of errors but from a magnificent response to them.*

As I write these words, I am sitting by a fire. The residue of a previous day spent with a favourite client clings to the fabric of this day's thoughts and feelings. I am watching the river in our back yard wind its way through an icy maze. The smell of bacon is wafting through the house and my children have found that rare moment of cooperation and peace. Later today we will trudge through the snow on our way to a family skating venture, watch a new movie that my kids have been nervously awaiting and enjoy an interesting conversation during dinner back home. We will complete our day's adventure with another long fire and the lazy thoughts of how good life can be.

The process of building a good fire has taken me some time to learn and is an apt metaphor for personal mastery. Last night, as crystals of fragile snow were falling into the darkness of an early winter's night, I spent considerable time splitting logs into the slender bits of kindling that would ease the next few fires. I made different sizes appropriate for the phases of a durable blaze. A small mess of the littlest pieces provides the basic foundation. As these catch and the heat builds in the stove box, I add the next size which spread the base and forms the first small coals. At just the right moment, as I am careful neither to overwhelm the tenuous build up of flames nor fall behind their bright lead, I place the larger pieces on. These form the final base of hot coals that give the larger logs the opportunity to make their contribution. A little preparation, some patience and a proven method and in no time the heat of a worthwhile enterprise warms the reaches of my body and soul. I have discovered through trial and much error that this way works best. It did not used to be this way.

I used to run my business and personal life the way I used to try to build fires: moving faster than I had earned the right to. I would often just throw the contents of a large bottle of gas on a poorly organized array of oversized logs, hoping desperately that it would start, just as I would aimlessly throw time, energy and money at a project. After an exciting explosion of energy, I would be left with a cool pile of logs no closer to releasing the warmth inside than before I lit the match. If I did manage to get it going, it would often slip away with my waning attention.

Making my life and business work has also taken some time. I have always been interested in the method of deliberate will: to conceive of a worthwhile and feasible idea for something and take it through all of its stages towards its full fruition. A good experience and positive result gained unconsciously are not as interesting to me as the same outcome earned consciously. Any dolt can start a forest fire. Much of what I have tried has not worked; some has worked brilliantly. I have experienced many sorts of business and personal failure: getting divorced, being fired by clients, authoring product flops and losing other people's money – all in the search of the method that works. At times I have found it: I have experienced the joy of winning design awards, making good money for investors, creating the kinds of things I am deeply proud of and earning a reputation for satisfying clients at a high level. This is the history from which I draw my future. My days proceed with the hard-won wisdom that came from a long apprenticeship of helping clients lose millions of dollars, helping clients make millions of dollars and learning the often subtle difference between the two.

My greatest achievement is this day. It is neither all that I am capable of nor my best work to date. I hope that tomorrow I will learn another valuable lesson to take me farther along the path. *Fulfillment is not the result of distantly-spaced and short-lived achievements but the experience of ideal days borne of patient, conscious design.*

For the Love of Service
Working a New Model for Enterprise

I spent the first part of my professional career as a produ
design consultant. The philosophies, technologies an
methodologies I learned during my apprenticeship in the world
of physical products became the basis for my passion for
services. Even the Master's thesis I wrote was on the design of
service businesses. Of all the projects that I was a part of, i t
was designing the design service itself that I found most
fulfilling and that I look back on with the most pride.

I love the idea of the service business: one human being
making life better for another human being. Services are the
most direct and intimate form of value creation. Retail
businesses, unless they are high-end are usually transactional
and focused on merchandise; information businesses are often
impersonal and lacking in spirit; manufacturing businesses
place an artificial physical item between maker and user. I
love the ways and means of service: enrolling clients into
vulnerable and intangible opportunities and then delivering
powerful, emotionally-rooted experiences and results.

When I approached author Jay Levinson with my first
book idea, my proposal was all about product development and
starting hard, product-based ventures. After three or four years
of writing, through dozens of drafts and during intensive
personal development work, I discovered a new idea for a
second book: the love-based business.

The first time I mentioned the words love and business
in the same sentence, the person laughed. When they realized
I was serious, they got very uncomfortable. It seems that love
has no business being in business and business has no love for
love. I knew I was on the verge of something big. When I told
Jay, he said, "Your first book will get published and be a good
book; your second will change the world." Years after that
dramatic piece of encouragement, I realized that I had written

id had shelved the first. You have it in your
᠁y was right, because I do intend to change

latest phase of my professional career, I have
coaching and assisting high-end professional
.trepreneurs in designing their ventures around their
.ues. In my work with these entrepreneurs, I make the
.t that the purpose of business is not to make money per se,
.id that the promise of being our own bosses, freedom and
flexibility are quickly replaced with commitments, stress,
billable hour quotas and the demands of clients, employees and
bankers. There has to be something more that drives us to
become entrepreneurs and keeps us engaged throughout the
inevitable periods of doubt, fear and hardship. I believe that
only love is that powerful. By love I do not mean romantic love,
the love between a boy and his dog or the love that's deified in
pop songs. I mean that positive, passionate part of who we are
that makes a contribution. By making my contribution, I am
expressing my love. This is the basis of all service. Our
contributions are the unique gifts we are to people and the
planet. When we make a contribution, people experience our
value. Our value helps make their worlds better places to be.

The purpose of my life and thus the purpose of my
business is to make my unique contribution to the group of people
I am most attracted to serving, in the way that works best for
all of us. The design of my business and how I operate, all the
technical and practical parts that actually make up my
practice, are simply the vehicle for me to express myself to the
people I love – my clients. Love is both my contribution and the
way I express it through my business. *Our best contributions to
our best people are really profound acts of love which improve
their worlds and make our ventures healthier, stronger and
capable making an even bigger difference.*

Every spring, my family heads out on our traditional camping trip to reconnect with our nature after a long winter. We travel to some remote mountain wilderness area, far from other more civilized campers and set up a three day retreat from the stresses of mundane city life. As we welcome in the new season, watching winter trying in vain to keep its futile hold on the changing landscape, we are free to ponder the deeper truths in our own changing lives.

On our first such excursion, my daughter Maren was four years old. Late one evening, during a rare respite from the driving wind and biting cold, she and I were wrapped around a blazing fire. I had been settling into a comfortable, languorous drowse, when my daughter casually announced that, "Daddy, I have thoughts that nobody knows about." At the edge of my consciousness, I detected a diversion from the normal kind of four-year old banter and perked up. She looked up into the starry night and stated with casual confidence, "it's weird isn't it...that we are alive and the universe is up there...I just haven't figured out yet why it all exists."

My daughter has always been bright, both intellectually and in her demeanour, but her apparent investigations into ontology and cosmogenesis took me quite by surprise. We discussed the nature of being and the universe, and I went to bed certain she would someday figure out how everything is connected and then explain it to me. Perhaps she already has it wired and is just patiently waiting to learn the words to describe it.

Although I would like to think that it has been my brilliant influence that has brought about her precocious spiritual and intellectual charm, in truth, she has always seemed to me to be an old soul. She has always seemed connected to the deeper realities of life. Maren has always brimmed with some interesting hidden purpose. At the end of her first year of school, in describing her approach to making friends, she mused, "at the start of school it is pretty easy to make friends, but if you wait until the end of the year to try to make friends with someone, it could take up to five minutes." When she was three, she was famous for her many kinds of hugs. At a large family gathering, when someone asked her for one, she announced that she had no more in her inventory at that moment. When I asked for one she said, "I always have one saved for my daddy." Although I have no idea what her future holds or what calling she will choose, it is clear to me that she is a special and unique person who makes a difference connecting to the people around her. She is here for a reason. And she knows it.

Observing children has given me richer insight and admiration into the whole enterprise of conducting life. There is so much more to being alive than merely growing up, choosing some mindless career, saving up as much money as possible and retiring in some arthritis-friendly part of Florida. There is the choice to make a difference. When my daughter gazed up at the sky that evening, with a glint of hope in her eyes, I am sure she was not looking at some worn path through life. I am convinced that she got some inkling of the great life she could have, that it was not merely a case of getting through it with as little pain and discomfort as possible. I think she knows she can choose precisely the path most meant for her, that she has the opportunity and all the gifts required to escape mediocrity and live an uncommon life. I dare not interfere in that choice or its prosecution. I only hope to guide it with some reverence. As human beings we all have the opportunity and choice to create what we want or cope with what we get. *The greatest gift that we have to give is the contribution we are alive to make.*

I charged four thousand dollars for my first professional design job. I had never received a check that large before and wanted to appreciate the magnitude of the event, so I cashed it in for two hundred twenty dollar bills. I took the large roll, held together by an elastic band, and placed the cash into neat piles on my table: this much for rent, this much for food, this much for savings and so on. I was immediately impressed by how massive that much cash looks like. I realized then, in sobering awe, that the client had placed their hard-earned, after-tax dollars in my care, in trust for a great result.

During a philosophy course in design school, we discussed the moral basis for profit. In the scenario, two people were stranded on a desert island. One of the shipwrecked survivors learned how to knock coconuts from the trees and crack them open to release the life-giving meat and milk. The other could not. Under such conditions, who has the right to the coconuts? Is the inventor of the "coconut technology" entitled to all of the coconuts? Should he share them with his starving partner? If so, should he share them equally or is he entitled to a premium as a reward for his invention?

I have come to appreciate that there are two certain paths to failure and unhappiness in business. The first is to do something solely for the money; the second is to avoid money entirely. If an entrepreneur selfishly pursues an opportunity solely on its financial merits, they can make "a killing", but might miss the deep passion that sustains them. If the entrepreneur selflessly pursues an opportunity based on its social or personal virtues, they might be inclined to see money as a corruption to their rectitude and shun success. I have met financially successful but unhappy entrepreneurs doing what they hate and apparently happy entrepreneurs following meaningful vocations who are starving and failing to make them work. The best path might be right between avarice and altruism – the path that unites the twin drives of making money and making a difference.

New England's Timberland Boot Company has done well by doing good. They have made lots of money selling boots and shoes, but also operate under a social mandate "pull on your boots and make a difference." Their manifesto is "to know your greatness, you must share it with someone who needs it", and they mean what they say. The premiums charged on the sales of its products not only enrich shareholders but support important causes by giving each of its employees massive paid leave every year to volunteer on important social projects.

I like the idea of getting paid well for what I would do for free anyway. I am happy making my contribution, discovering my values and expressing them through my business. As I make these work well for my clients, I become successful and they pay me well in return. I then take the proceeds and take care of myself, my causes and the people important to me. I create meaningful new products and spend myself living up to the promise of value my life has for me and the people I serve.

Growing companies with important visions deserve to profit by fulfilling their missions. Business leaders have a duty of fiduciary trust to protect the interests of the shareholders and the firm's high-value clients deserve the same consideration as other investors. These dedicated people use their hard-earned cash to purchase the company's products at a premium and are thereby the source of the firm's profits. I am willing to remain a committed customer if I sense that a company is using the premium I pay it for worthy purposes. If the company betrays the integrity of their values or fails to live up to their purpose on too many occasions, I may remove my support. *Ethical profit is both a company's reward for its ingenuity and a statement by its employees, investors and customers of their commitment to the more noble purpose and values at the heart of the enterprise.*

Commercial Information

Thank you for taking the time to read this book. My company, Venture Guiding Inc. is an entrepreneurial design and coaching business. I am passionate about assisting service professionals in structuring their ventures for higher purpose and higher profit. I offer a modular venture development program to assist entrepreneurs in reducing stress and making a meaningful change in the way they do business and life.

I am in business to make ventures work better for entrepreneurs and the world around them. My long term vision is to build a community of entrepreneurial activists working together to enhance their wealth, the quality of life for their people and the sustainability of the natural environment we all share. The community is called the *Venture Association*.

For information on my coaching and speaking services, to offer feedback on this book of any sort, request a free sample of my work or inquire about joining the *Venture Association*, please contact me at:

www.ventureguiding.com

keith@ventureguiding.com

To receive the free Venture Guiding weekly on-line column go to:

www.ventureguiding.com/column/subscribe

For information on Guerrilla Marketing products and services contact:

www.gmarketing.com

Index of Personal Values

acceptance
achievement
alignment
authenticity
care
collaboration
completion
contribution
courage
desire
empowerment
enrichment
esteem
exploration
flow
generosity
growth
inclusion
innovation
integration
joy
legacy
optimism
power
reliability
revelation
spirituality
transformation
validation
vision

accord
acknowledgment
allowance
balance
co-operation
community
congruence
control
creativity
duty
enhancement
enthusiasm
excellence
fairness
focus
grace
honesty
influence
insight
integrity
justice
love
order
purpose
resolution
service
stability
truth
variety
vitality

accountability
actualization
ambition
beauty
coherence
competence
consciousness
conviction
deference
elegance
enjoyment
equity
expedition
flexibility
fulfillment
greatness
humour
ingenuity
inspiration
intensity
kindness
meaning
perseverence
refinement
responsibility
sincerity
tolerance
uniqueness
visibility
zeal

Index of Economic Values

agreement
comfort
consensus
energy
growth
margins
ownership
productivity
quality
retention
satisfaction
strength
volume

approval
competence
consistency
fitness
health
momentum
persistence
profit
reliability
revenue
security
validation
wealth

cashflow
completion
efficiency
goodwill
knowledge
morale
price
progress
reputation
sales
speed
vitality
wellness

Higher Purpose, Higher Profit

Acknowledgments

I never quite understood why people at awards ceremonies would stand up in front of the world and thank everyone including their dog and their second grade teacher. That was before I sat down to write this section and came to appreciate the magnitude of the contributions I have received from so many people. I do not remember who my second grade teach was, but I liked her too. And I have great dogs.

I spent many of my early adult years torturing the English language and the many brave souls curious enough or dedicated enough to come in contact with anything I had to say or write. Although the process of becoming a writer is one that I expect will continue until the moment of my passing, I owe a large debt to a large community of people who have encouraged, and in some cases kindly tolerated, my efforts so far.

My largest debt is to Jay Levinson, who has been the purest kind of mentor. I phoned him out of the blue on a cold November morning in 1995, at his home in the perfectly acclimated town of San Rafael, and asked him to write a book with me. He said yes. And lucky for me, we have not written a book together because he has become someone more important than a coauthor. His acknowledgment and encouragement have helped to keep me on the path during the many times I have wanted to bail on the enterprise: "you are just in the 'nobody wants to listen to what I have to say' phase of becoming a writer; I am looking forward to your second book." I am grateful also to Mike Larsen, Jay's agent, who was kind and patient enough to show me what the gate to the New York publishers looked like and what standard I would have to make to get to the show.

The polish of this book belongs to the elegant design of Janine MacKinnon, the astute editing of Wendy Ross and the clever work of Gwen Gades and the folks at Blitzprint.

My "big word" phase of writing began with Dixon Thompson, who vouched for my brain as entry to design school, and continued, and I wish I could say finished, with my thesis and supervisors Jim O'Grady and Ed McMullan and Peter Robinson who patiently supported me as I chased my intellectual tale through a written document intelligible only by me and barely by them.

Professional writing started with an opportunity to write a monthly column for Luke Vorstermans, a keen editor who wisely gave me only 600 words a month to play with. Indeed, I could not get in to too much trouble with only a handful of paragraphs. I fell in love with the short essay column format and the challenge of developing an idea, sharply in a short time, with an economy of words. I wrote some for the Calgary Herald (thanks to Ron Nowell) and one of my coaching clients Lee Waterman suggested a collection of these columns might make for a good book. I abandoned the twentieth draft of a previous manuscript I was working on and this book was borne. I appreciate dee Hobsbawn-Smith, a great chef and food author, for convincing me that I had delicious prose inside of me and that I could take it out if I wanted to.

Any one thing is the result of a series of many moments and interactions and this thing is no exception. Nothing good gets done by itself and every new creative thing can only fill the space created by the people who support it. The work that appears in this volume did not emerge from some sequestered writing project. Most of my ideas come either from the reading and speaking I do or from the great conversations I have had with the hundreds of entrepreneurs I have had the good fortune to work with. Many of them have been experimental subjects, letting me try out many of the ideas in this book. Thanks to Craig Riley for being the first client to entrust me with actual cash, my first few coaching clients Steve Kaltenhauser and Tannis Bilkoski and the rest of my client roster, allies and friends of the past four years: Rob Allendorf, David Andruko, Judy Atkinson, Lori Atkinson, Annette Aubrey, Stefan

Baldwinson, Laura Ballerini, Colette Bennett, Darren Biedermann, Steve Bommer, Niel Bosdat, Wayne Boss, Wes Bot, Tim Breithaupt, Graham Bruce, Rod Burns, Michael Burns, Jeff Bush, Dean Christie, Marjorie Contenti, Brian Copping, Todd Costella, Terry Crooks, Bill Cryderman, Ted Dare, Scott Darling, Bill Darling, Kent Davidson, Dave Dial, John Duhault, Eva Duncan, Medy Dytuco, Ian Elliott, Gord Elser, Clarke Erwin, Thomas Fahey, Cory Fiset, Jay Fiset, Joan Flemmer, Peter Garry, Gary Goemans, Roger Grant, Rob Gryba, Barry Hart, Susi Hately-Aldous, Jason Hay, Glen Hay, dee Hobsbawn-Smith, Karin Hoernig, Debra Hughes, Jim Jamieson, Shel Jacobsen, Brian Johnston, David Johnstone, Gloria Jones, Sharon Kaczkowski, Shellan Kinvig, Dwayne Klassen, Rhondalynn Korolak, Randy Koroluk, Jaret Leah, Maggie Leal-Valias, Terry Libin, Mary Livingstone, Clive Llewellyn, Karen Lukcas, Valerie MacLeod, Sheri MacMillan, Jim Maldaner, Sharlene Massie, Ian Matheson, Mark McCulloch, Cam McIntosh, Doug McNabb, Ross McNichol, Bryce Medd, Fred Mertz, John Milner, Elissa Miskey, Grant Molyneux, Peter Morris, Barry Morris, Gayle Morton, Ted Murdoch, Linda Nummela, John O'Donnell, Wendy Olson, Marcia Oro, Russ Oro, Mara Osis, Brian Paterson, Tim Phillips, Jason Pocza, Irfana Qureshi, Trina Read, Steve Remmington, Vincent Robichaud, David Romanzin, Bernard Rousseau, Bill Rutledge, Carol Sadler, Chad Sartison, David Saxby, Patty Schachter, Trent Schumann, Patty Shortreed, Don Smith, Bill Stemp, Michael Stern, Nan Stevenson, Peter Stewart, George Stewart, Gary Sykes, Harry Taylor, Martin Thomas, Hal Thompson, Tim Thorpe, Peter Tilma, Blaine Treloar, Steve Vail, Karey Van Buren, Craig Van Dongen, Linda Vavra-Roberts, Peter Vodak, Steven Walker, Adrienne Waller, Bill Watt, Lee Waterman, Don Wensrich, Alice Wheaton, James White, Michael Whitt, Nick Wight, Wayne Yager, Cal Zaryski and Sean Young.

There is a large group of partners and supporters I have worked with in the past thirteen years. I am honoured to have been in any small way a part of all of their lives and I am glad they have been in mine. I am grateful to Randy Revell for his wisdom and teachings. Even now, I am only vaguely aware of the influence his life has had on me through both the programs I have taken from his company and the personal and business time we have spent together. I am grateful to my team of coaches and advisors who have helped to keep me moving forward: Phil Holcomb for his encouragement and patient coaxing out of my personal accountability, Brian Copping for introducing me back into the flow, Grant Molyneux for a comfortable and balanced approach to everything, Brian Johnston for an intense one, Harry Taylor for being the first cool accountant I could talk about my life passion with, Chad Sartison for convincing me that money is my friend, Rod Burns for his reminders of where I have been as I figure out where I am going, Dan Haygeman for being the kind of facilitator I aspire to be, Debi Andrus for an unendingly interesting conversation about the interrelationship between innovation and spirituality, Peter Stewart for reminding me that I could always do better than get stuck with some compromise, Hal Thompson for introducing me to the breadth of the entrepreneurial profession, Peter Holmes for showing me the patient approach to business development, David Beckwermert for reminding me that the different types of cash in and cash out are in fact quite different, Ron Stickley for his sense about how to fit anything into a market, Ross Drysdale for his quiet confidence, Rick Burley for pointing out that I had actually become a successful coach, Phil Shragge for teaching me how to stand up to strong-minded entrepreneurs, Javan Belcourt for making sure my head is always right and Trina Read for making sure my presentation is always right. Many thanks to Shawn Lucas, Tim Goodison, Carole Perkins, Tammy Armstrong, Nicole Hildebrandy, Andrea Hamm, Roland Robichaud, Brian Johns, Marisa Garcia and the rest of the team of people from the Bow Valley Club who smooth out all of my business dealings there.

Thanks to my goal setting group for being cool guys who have enough self-confidence to hug in public: Steve Kaltenhauser, Trent Schumann and Todd Costella.

Thanks to the collaborations with Margot Loveseth for being the perfect mother to my kids and one of the best small business managers I know, Barry Wylant for the sharpness of his intellect and designer's hand, Peter Morris for his direct honesty, John Sobota for his awe in life, Ken Jackson for his backbone, Kim McMullen for her integrity, Debra Hughes for her courage and Jason Hay for being a person who I have discovered can find a reason to be happy about anything.

I am grateful to Donna and Rick Sukovieff for patiently helping our family to remain living in the most beautiful place in the world.

I almost ended up as an electrician, and while that would have been a noble pursuit it would not have been the most efficient way to express my point of view. I thank my high school electricity teacher and then most frequent climbing partner Norm Sigalet for the thoughtful intervention he made to lead me to the path of university and entrepreneurship and for making sure I got to out climbing to when I was too poor in school to get out on my own.

I cannot find the words to thank Karl Nagy, who, while gone in the physical sense, will not be forgotten in the spiritual.

Lastly to my family. I appreciate Tony and Jane Crane for having such a cool daughter and letting me keep her at home during critical times for this book or our business. I am grateful to my father Cliff for his way with words, to my mother Margaret for her way with people, my brother Warren and sister Shelley for their ways with the world and my wife Tania for choosing a way with me.